*Ideas are not only interesting, but consider this...
they can change our culture, change our
understanding, and help us adjust to the world and society.*

In the Middle Ages, there was a general belief that almost all significant ideas had come from the ancients. To be educated you had to have learned what Socrates, Galen, and other recognized sages had revealed. Although we have learned a lot from studying history, new ideas as well as those in the past are changing the way we live.

Combining information from many sources leads us to new ways of thinking. Can we convince our youth that appreciation of the ideas that came from the past, combined with the innovations of the present, will reveal a new reality? Possibly new concepts that will make life better for us all?

Richard Holmes, author of an interesting book *Age of Wonder*, said, "Scientific discoveries are as unexpected and interesting as poetry. The boundless prodigality of nature inspired scientists and poets with the same feelings of wonder." I feel the same way about ideas, which lead to discoveries in science, in society, in business, and in our understanding of each other.

About the Author

Dr. Myrvin Ellestad has built a life worthy of respect and admiration, both in his professional career and in his personal endeavors. In addition to being in the forefront of heart-related medical developments, he has enjoyed membership in many prestigious medical organizations, won awards too numerous to list here, and served in top positions in hospitals and university faculties. An octogenarian as of this writing, he remains very active in his personal and professional life. Dr. Ellestad lives in Southern California with his wife and large family of grown children and grandchildren.

A ROMANCE WITH IDEAS

A ROMANCE WITH IDEAS

The Time for Thinking Has Come

MYRVIN H. ELLESTAD

CEDAR VISTA
Los Angeles, CA

Copyright © 2012 by Myrvin H. Ellestad

Cedar Vista Books
Los Angeles, CA
www.cedarvistapublishing.com

All rights reserved. No part of this book may be reproduced or transmitted in any form or by any means, electronic or mechanical, including photocopying, recording, or by any information storage and retrieval system, except in the case of brief quotations embodied in critical articles and reviews, without prior written permission of the publisher.

Although the author and publisher have made every effort to ensure the accuracy and completeness of information contained in this book, we assume no responsibility for errors, inaccuracies, omissions, or any inconsistency herein.

Printed in the United States of America

ISBN Paperback: 978-0-9858525-0-4
ISBN e-book: 978-0-9858525-1-1

Book Consultant: Ellen Reid
Book Cover & Interior Design: Ghislain Viau

Dedicated to my loving wife, Lera. I depend on her continued support and encouragement.

Contents

Foreword	xv
Introduction	1

Section I: The Birthplace of Ideas

Where Do Ideas Come From?	5
The Definition of an Idea	7
Ideas about Intellectual and Social Progress	8
Exaptation	12
Tinkering	12
Curiosity Is the Craving for Reason and New Experiences—Marco Polo	13
Lateral Thinking	14
The Utility of Error	16
The Importance of Innovation	16
Theoretical Studies of Innovation	18
Mathematics Is Reality	19
Xenophilia	20
The Need to Categorize	21
Science and Philosophy	21
Historical Belief Systems	23
Confucius from the Heart	24

Section II: Ideas Throughout History (Medical Breakthroughs)

William Harvey	27
The Stethoscope – Laennec	29

Heart Catheterization – Forssman 29
Coronary Angiography – Sones 31
Afterload Reduction in Heart Failure 32
Chronotrophic Incompetence 34
Pacemakers – Greatbatch 36
Smallpox – Edward Jenner 38

Other Breakthroughs

The Earth Rotates Around the Sun – Copernicus 40
The Printing Press – Gutenberg 41
Evolution – Darwin 42
Alternative Views on Evolution 45
Genetics – Gregor Mendel 47
Braille 49
Dynamite – Nobel 49
Sputnik – Guier & Wiffenbach 50
Superconductivity – Onnes 51
Belief and the Brain 52
The Idea of Democracy 53

Section III: Ideas Today

Techonomy – Social Power 55
Socialism vs. Capitalism 56
The Evolution of Smarts 58
The Curse of Administration 59
The Credit for Discoveries 61
The Prevalence of Unscientific Beliefs 62
The Belief in God Today 62
How to Explain the Belief Systems of
    Educated People 65
The Evolution of Ideas 67
Innovation in Business and Life 68

Some Theoretical Studies on Innovation	71
Steve Jobs: The Idea Man	72
The Emergence of Grandparents	74
The Influence of Social Hierarchy	74
The Progress of Humanity, Maybe	75
Interpersonal Behavior	77
Some Ideas About Our Culture	78

Section IV: The Future of Ideas

A Global Government	81
The Death of Common Sense	84
Economics – The Bourgeois Virtue	86
The Rush to the Cities	90
Education and the Significance of Life	92
Understanding Islam	94
Reconsidering Benevolence	95

Appendix and Essays

Appendix #1	99
Appendix #2	101
Appendix #3: Facts and Ideas from Anywhere – William C. Roberts	101
Essays	
The Need to Suffer	102
The Greeks Started All the Trouble…	
The Cult of Individualism	112
Conformity: The Societal Prison	119
Conclusions	125
Books	127
Acknowledgments	131

Foreword

There comes a time in life when the urge to leave something of himself to those he knew, to those he worked with, and to those he loved over the years becomes increasingly powerful. As I considered the possibility that it would be worthwhile to jot down some ideas that might interest or influence my readers. I realized that what I had to say was a composite of what I had learned from my experiences, what I had read, and I was influenced by people I admired who were prolific authors and brilliant scientists.

Some people explore and write about far-off places, unusual cultures, famous celebrities, and political events. I have decided to write about ideas. Ideas that have fascinated me for years, some of which most people may not have given much thought.

Ever since I was very young, I enjoyed asking questions. Questions about people, about science, about why we believe the way we do. This trait led to the accumulation of all sorts of ideas, which I propose to share with you. Trying to understand the reasons for things has always been enjoyable and a few times has allowed me to make some contributions to the practice of cardiology, which has added to the satisfaction I have received from my sixty years of practice. Some of these contributions will be described later.

In 1980, the *Encyclopedia Britannica* published a yearbook of science. They described recent progress in over 46 areas; from forestry and mining, from psychiatry to archeology, from computers to mathematics, from aircraft to chemistry. Just think how much progress has been made since then. Each time progress is made it is preceded by an idea. I believe this book illustrates how important ideas have become in our society. In this little book I will examine a few ideas that have changed the way we think, the way we live, and how we interact with the world around us.

In the early part of my career, I spent a short time in the pulmonary department of the University of California in San Francisco, headed by Julius Comroe, who was at that time recognized as one of the most outstanding pulmonary physiologists in the country. A few years after my visit, he published one of my favorite books entitled *Retrospectroscope, Insights Into Medical Discovery*. This interesting book, published in 1957, is, in my mind, one of the most unusual and informative collections of medical history, and I must admit that my book

Foreword

is somewhat similar, although it examines the history of much more than medicine.

The ideas I will relate have altered my worldview and, as you read on, they may alter some of your beliefs as well. As you will find in many of the stories, combining the ideas you learned from history or the experiences of colleagues solves problems that were difficult. They often led to new insights that, in retrospect, seemed obvious, while before the combinations were a mystery.

Someone once said, *"If you quote one author it is plagiarism, but if you quote many authors it is research."* Combining previously described ideas with a new observation is progress. The more ideas one has, the more likely they will come together in some meaningful way.

This book will present many ideas that have changed our lives. Maybe one of them will change yours.

Introduction

It will be apparent that unconventional and unique ideas have influenced historical events, and we will examine many of these ideas in detail.

In order to appreciate my claims, it is important to explain something about my background. I was raised in a small mountain town in Northern California by parents who were both schoolteachers. We went to church every Sunday in a little Methodist church, and I also attended Sunday school where I learned quite a lot about the Bible. We knew almost everyone in this little town of 2,000 people.

My parents were quite conventional, although my father, who was born in Northern Minnesota of a Norwegian family, believed in plenty of hard work. Besides teaching auto mechanics in the local high school, he built houses on weekends and during vacations, and I was expected to help. It seemed I always had more chores to do than the other kids. I raised rabbits and goats and helped with my parents' chickens and vegetable garden.

Probably, because of my mother's influence, I became a nonstop reader as early as age seven. One of the books that was emphasized was the Bible and, before too long, I began to question what seemed to be some of its contradictions and also some of the stories I heard from the preacher.

One of the biblical claims, that the world was created in seven days, did not fit with some of the science books I was beginning to read. By the time I was in high school, I had read most of the Old Testament. Although the Christians taught that we should love our neighbors, it did not seem to fit with the Bible story where God told Joshua to go into Jericho and kill every man, woman, and child, as well as their oxen and sheep. This might have been the first recorded genocide.

My days at U.C. Berkeley were an awakening for a country boy, a name given to me by my city-raised fraternity brothers. My first girlfriend was a cute, very bright Jewish girl I met in chemistry class who, I discovered, was unacceptable at our fraternity parties. My resistance to their anti-Semitism probably was the reason I was labeled as a nonconformist, a label I did not seem to mind even then.

For a boy brought up in a conservative family, the radicalism of Berkeley was a new experience. Almost every day

Introduction

there was a gathering of a group who believed in communism. The sister of the brilliant head of the physics department, Oppenheimer, was the chairman of the local Communist party. However, Oppenheimer, some time after he developed our famous atomic bomb, denied he had ever joined the party. As I look back, being a nonconformist probably also made me a skeptic so that I could never believe in most of the radical ideas so common on the Berkeley campus in the early '40s. My experiences in medical school, followed by two years in the Navy, mostly spent in the Naval Hospital in Guantanamo Bay, Cuba, provided the opportunity to come away with many ideas that were unconventional by the standards of the day. Thus, my love of ideas is not new and I hope my readers will find them as fascinating as I have. I will review some ideas that have changed our lives as early as the Middle Ages, but I promise to change them even more so in the future.

By the time I was in college it was apparent to me that not only the Bible, but also many dogmatic statements by so-called authorities, might be in error. This skeptical state of mind was not very popular with some of my friends, but somehow it was quite satisfying. It often stimulated me to inquire about concepts that were, in some groups, very unpopular.

One day my roommate in our fraternity house, Hilary Crawford, invited me to have dinner with his family in San Francisco. On arriving in the early afternoon at their beautiful home in St. Francis Woods, I found I was about an hour early.

A Romance with Ideas

To pass the time I reviewed the newspapers in their living room and much to my surprise they had copies of the *Daily Worker*, the newspaper put out by the Communist party. When Mr. Crawford, a very successful attorney, arrived home, I remarked that I was surprised that he was a Communist. He laughed and remarked, "I'm definitely not a Communist, but in my business it pays to keep in touch with the ideas of those you disagree with." Mr. Crawford was not only a successful attorney, but also a civic leader in San Francisco. At that time he was president of the Commonwealth Club, one of the most prestigious organizations in California. Because he was a recognized leader in San Francisco, his remarks made an indelible impression and reinforced the tendency to ask questions and try to examine both sides of the issues.

At this point we will embark on an analysis of ideas and events that I believe have been important in the evolution of our cultural and scientific surroundings.

Section I

The Birthplace of Ideas

WHERE DO IDEAS COME FROM?

It is popular to believe that new ideas appear out of the blue or in a flash of understanding. An example of this is when Isaac Newton discovered gravity. The story goes that he was sitting under an apple tree, an apple fell, and he suddenly conceived that gravity, a force that was manifested all the way from the heavenly bodies to the earth, would explain everything.

It will become evident that although there may be times when this occurs, most ideas come from other ideas. This was certainly true of Newton, who invented calculus and other new concepts and knew a lot about many things.

Those who have a broad knowledge in many areas are the ones who usually generate new ideas—often from putting

A Romance with Ideas

together their awareness of the present with established concepts previously described. Steven Johnson, who did an early study of innovative ideas, found that they almost always came from cities where people came together to share information rather than from rural areas where people rarely communicated. Exceptions to this occasionally occur but almost always where different cultures mix. More about cities later.

Some questions I will try to answer: (1) Are innovations accidental discoveries? (2) Are there environments that lead to ideas and innovation? (3) What type of people become innovators?

A term that has been used to describe innovation is serendipity. This comes from a Persian fairy tale "Three Princes of Serendip." They were always making discoveries by accident and sagacity. How important is serendipity? A number of authors have published works dealing with this question and their answers warrant our consideration.

We all know a good idea when we see one after it has been accepted and proven to be useful; i.e., the printing press, the pencil, the flush toilet, the battery, Google, and on and on. The rapid increase since about the mid-1800s has been written about and analyzed by many authors. It has been explained by the change in the economics of modern times, by the dramatic increase in education, by the proximity of innovators in cities, and concentrations of people who contribute to scientific advance. Not only does communication between innovative people facilitate this process, but also

Section I: The Birthplace of Ideas

populations of people who are ready to try new inventions and ideas play a role.

A recent article in the *New Yorker* pointed out that some populations are more ready to try out new devices. Buying new products is often risky, but by accepting risks the usefulness can be established. Americans have for generations been more prone to accept these risks. American farmers have led the way in adopting genetically modified crops. After Henry Ford pioneered the assembly line, the American public by 1920 bought 2 million cars annually, accounting for 90% of the world's cars. Appliances, like electric irons and vacuum cleaners, were commonplace in American households by 1920 when they were still rare in the rest of the civilized world. By 1960 American airlines were proving 60% of the world's travel.

As it turns out, innovation requires creative people and a population always ready to try out new devices or new ways of doing things. Will other countries acquire our habit? Probably, eventually.

THE DEFINITION OF AN IDEA

"If nature has made any one thing less susceptible than all others of exclusive property, it is the action of the thinking power called an idea, which an individual may exclusively possess as long as he keeps it to himself; but the moment it is divulged, it forces itself into the possession of everyone and the receiver cannot dispossess himself of it. He who receives an idea from me receives instructions himself without lessening mine; as he who lights his taper at mine receives light without darkening me. The ideas should be spread over the globe, for the moral and mutual instructions of man. This seems to have been benevolently designed by nature," Thomas Jefferson said (1743–1826).

Richard Dawkins claimed that ideas are like DNA in that they carry information. He invented the term "Meme" (a mnemonic gene). Although all ideas don't have that capacity, as many are soon forgotten, the ones discussed in my story will not be forgotten and will fit Dawkins' description. They often have been the source of information that has changed the way we think, the way we live. These are the ideas, or memes, that are featured in the pages to follow.

IDEAS ABOUT INTELLECTUAL AND SOCIAL PROGRESS

In ancient Greece, a group of scholars, the Pythagoreans, held that nature should be investigated purely for the sake of disinterested knowledge and not for any practical reward. They were probably the first to use the term "philophia" to mean the love of wisdom for its own sake. Pythagoreans claimed that some men were slaves of ambition, some of money, but there were a special few whose interest was in acquiring knowledge. Plato was certainly one with this idea. In his *Timaeus*, he claimed, "He who has been earnest in his

Section I: The Birthplace of Ideas

love of knowledge and of true wisdom must have thoughts that are immortal and divine."

It is interesting that when they discovered that the tone produced by the string of the monochord—a very early stringed instrument—could be determined by measuring the length of the string, they decided that numbers were divine, a concept probably shared by mathematicians and physicists even today.

Euripides claimed that many creatures failed to survive because they were unsuited to do so, leaving only those well suited. I wonder if Darwin knew about Euripides' claim that preceded his idea by 2,000 years.

When the Catholic Church became socially powerful, it squelched independent thought for centuries. However, Gutenberg and his printing press began to overcome the suppression. In 1440, there were approximately 30,000 books in Europe, all hand copied almost exclusively by monks. By the year 1500, sixty years later, there were nine million. The church had lost control of publishing.

Although Copernicus had claimed the sun, not the earth, was the center of the universe in 1548, he was largely ignored, but by the time Galileo made this claim, so many more people had books and could read, thus the idea became such a threat to church dogma that he was placed on house arrest for the rest of his life. It is of interest that Martin Luther, hearing of

A Romance with Ideas

Copernicus' claim, called him a fool. But by 1620 the Catholic Church had forbidden their people the right to read the writing of both Copernicus and Galileo. The newly acquired ability to read was what probably stimulated the intellectual firmament that produced the Renaissance. Leonardo da Vinci (1452—1519) advised people to learn anatomy, physiology, and mathematics. "Do not rely on secondhand accounts. It is safer to study nature." He even designed a helicopter, but as far as it is known, he never built one.

Amerigo Vespucci, after visiting the new land discovered by Christopher Columbus, wrote extensively about it so that it was eventually named after him. Columbus was stimulated to sail west by the reports of riches in the new world by the writings of Marco Polo.

By this time Charlemagne had conquered most of Europe and encouraged scholars to translate the ancient Greek writings into Latin. At the same time, the population was increasing and as trade and commerce grew, people moved to the towns and cities. The cities promoted education outside the church, and the ideas of the Arab scholars became available. Thus, by 1600, intellectual ideas began to promote all sorts of knowledge. By this time Erasmus wrote a story called "The Prince," which emphasized that royalty as well as ordinary men often ignored moral principles. Much later the pioneering work of Thomas Edison that brought electricity to everybody empowered the world. Even from space the earth glows from

Section I: The Birthplace of Ideas

electric light. Next, the steam engine provided power for manufacturing and travel.

What made all of our inventions available to almost everybody? Corporations. By combining the funds of millions of investors, the technology resulting from thousands of inventions provided items manufactured at a cost that even the unemployed and those on welfare could afford. The financial rewards are also a powerful stimulus to invent new devices, new products, and new information that have dramatically altered civilization.

The motor of growth used to be land and natural resources. Today it is innovation, education, and economics. Benjamin Franklin, our first and last scientist statesman, said, "This generation may be the most important in history. They have the power to move us forward into a friendlier world. However, too many still adhere to primitive beliefs based on religion and other cultural-based prejudices. We only hope they will find a way to overcome these barriers." Today, over 200 years later, I believe his concerns still are important. However, the sudden increase in communication based on the Internet and the spread of a global language (English) will be a mechanism that will facilitate progress in the foreseeable future.

Isaac Asimov once said, "The saddest aspect of our society is that we are gathering knowledge much faster than we are gathering wisdom." Let us hope the amazing progress that has occurred continues in both categories—knowledge and wisdom.

EXAPTATION

This term, meaning to substitute, was probably invented by Steven J. Gould who was a brilliant biologist and who, in 1971, applied it to Gutenberg's use of the wine press to publish Bibles for the first time in quantities that made reading popular in Europe. Gould also used this term to describe how feathers on dinosaurs, which kept them warm, led to the archaeopteryx as it probably used the feathers to facilitate gliding. These feathers then evolved to facilitate flight in modern birds.

Exaptation is everywhere. In the early 1800s a French weaver named Joseph-Marie Jacquard developed punch cards to weave complex silk patterns. Charles Babbage borrowed the idea to program his analytical engine, the forerunner of the computer.

The history of the worldwide web of computers is a story of continuous exaptation. Francis Crick claims his recognition of the structure of DNA was an exaptation of ideas explored in long conversations with other investigators, including James Watson. They also relied on the X-ray photographs of DNA made by Rosalind Franklin in another lab, also at Cambridge in the United Kingdom.

TINKERING

Marcus Wohlsen, author of the interesting book *Biopunk*, claims that innovative people need to tinker. He gives examples where tinkering resulted in major breakthroughs, such as Steve

Section I: The Birthplace of Ideas

Jobs, who was the driving force behind the fabulously successful computer company, Apple. There seems little doubt that tinkering by brilliant, creative people pays off. On the other hand, an awful lot of people tinker and enjoy it without making any major breakthroughs. Also, tinkering results in adaptations where known information is used to make new progress. Watson & Crick were brilliant tinkerers. They used the X-ray crystallography of Rosalind Franklin. Their description of the structure of DNA netted them the Nobel Prize and opened up a whole new science that probably will change all of our lives.

For many people tinkering is fun. It satisfies curiosity, which at times is what induces people to create things and come up with ideas that can change our way of life and thought. Even when tinkering fails to produce anything useful it should be encouraged. Even negative information is often useful.

CURIOUSITY IS THE CRAVING FOR REASON AND NEW EXPERIENCES—MARCO POLO

Curiosity has driven men from as far back as history has been recorded. It drives men and many animals to seek answers that could better explain the events around us. In curiosity there is a ruthless element that can propel us to leave behind the safety of convention, to strike out in search of new ideas, cultures, and experiences. It is likely that curiosity drives achievement in many areas, especially science, history, and unconventional areas. It is very likely one of the forces that has led to the advanced culture we now enjoy. Curiosity was certainly the reason Marco Polo went to the Orient, and when he came home he was imprisoned for his curiosity.

In 1217, probably stimulated by his father's stories of his travels to the Far East, at the age of seventeen Marco set out to see for himself. His travels were translated by John Lerner of Glasgow University in 1999, but the original story, dictated shortly after his return to Genoa in 1298 while he was languishing in prison, altered history.

During his seventeen years of working for the Mongol emperor, Kublai Khan, as an emissary to many parts of the Orient, he learned to speak and write at least three foreign languages and probably was an astute observer of local customs and beliefs. When he returned home, his stories changed the prevailing attitude about China and the Far East. Prior to his trip it had been believed in the Western world that people in the East were very primitive. His stories about the fabulous wealth were no doubt what stimulated Columbus to set sail across the Atlantic expecting to bring home riches from the Orient. This story highlights how one man's brilliance and achievements can change the course of history. All too often we fail to appreciate the curious nonconformists who contribute so much.

LATERAL THINKING

Logic tends to direct most of us into "vertical thinking," a term used in a recent book by Edward de Bono, who points

Section I: The Birthplace of Ideas

out that the vertical process will occasionally fail to produce the best answers. In fact, some of the most creative people use lateral thinking. What does this mean?

As we assemble facts to arrive at the conclusion to a problem, we usually come up with the right, or best, answer. This direct approach is usually the most effective, but not always. Lateral thinking is a term for examining some of the least likely answers. Although statistically most of these will lead to the wrong answer, occasionally an unlikely solution turns out to be very useful. Perhaps even the best answer.

This technique is especially useful in generating new ideas. One has to say, although everyone knows this to be a fact, maybe there are exceptions. The previously stated aphorism, "examining what everyone knows to be true, and seeing something no one has seen before," is a type of lateral thinking.

De Bono claims that lateral thinking is especially useful to those who are creative, and as we know, creative people are in the minority. It appears also that lateral thinking is also uncommon. But as we examine the rapid evolution of technology, lateral thinking is much more common than it was in the past, partly because so many more people are exchanging ideas. Also, new ideas are more in vogue than in the past.

We can all remember when the smartest people were those who knew more about history, and about what famous people in the past believed. Although today fewer people learn about the past, this also means they are more likely to make the mistakes that history proved were destructive. Thus, knowledge of history is very useful. So we should, under most circumstances, study history so as not to repeat the mistakes that have proved destructive, but also be able to think "outside of the box," unconventionally, to use *lateral thinking*.

THE UTILITY OF ERROR

We now know that without error our DNA will always produce exact copies. Thus, life would not have evolved. However, because DNA does make errors, some of the new copies became better adapted to the environment and thus were more successful and reproduced. These errors have driven evolution, resulting in the process that has led to the dominance of Homo sapiens. If we can learn from errors, like our DNA, we can continue to make progress.

Some people refuse to accept that they have made mistakes. The most reluctant are politicians and the very religious. Most, but not all, scientists learn from their mistakes. Businessmen soon learn that mistakes usually cause financial pain, so they also learn from mistakes. Someday maybe everyone will learn from mistakes. It's probably a long way off.

THE IMPORTANCE OF INNOVATION

A recent issue of *Forbes*, probably the most popular weekly magazine among American businessmen, featured a significant

Section I: The Birthplace of Ideas

part of their first thirty pages to fifty businesses judged to be the most innovative. It is no surprise that these companies were also the most profitable, with income growth in the last few years reported from 75% to just under 50%. The products they provide are high-tech manufacturing, innovative retailing, and, of course, providers of computer-generated products, such as Apple and Google. It has been said that modern businesses are like *Alice In Wonderland's* red queen. They have to run fast to stay in the same place.

Usually the people who provide innovation are those who have a broad knowledge of not only the business they are working in but also other businesses and often history. They usually ask a lot of questions and are unconventional in their thought processes. They are not afraid to try ideas that fail. It has been said they think "outside of the box." There are a few who innovate year after year, even into their senior years, but these are rare birds. A study presented at the Skeptic Society, a group from Cal Tech that I enjoy, reported that new ideas almost never come from full-time professors in universities. In fact, it is common for them to claim new ideas are invalid. *"What I don't know isn't knowledge."* Later I will relate a story about the treatment of heart failure that was rejected by the chief of medicine at UCLA.

In spite of many people feeling uncomfortable with innovation, it seems to be accelerating every year. Maybe we all should relish in the progress and run as fast as we can to keep up.

THEORETICAL STUDIES OF INNOVATION

A whole host of books have been written about innovation. One of my favorites is *The Innovator's DNA*, by Dyer Gregerson and Clayton Christensen. First of all, innovators need to be disruptive. Consider the case of Steve Jobs, believed by *Forbes Magazine* and *Harvard Business Review* to be the best performing CEO in the United States and maybe even the world. Jobs was unconventional and certainly disruptive. Before Jobs, all computers had a fan to cool the heat generated by the power supply. He found an eccentric engineer, Rod Holt, who build a power supply that didn't need a fan and made it a feature of Apple computers. He also wanted a better way to control the data and added the mouse. He was an expert at constructive ways to be disruptive.

Secondly, innovators use associative thinking. One author called this the Medici Effect. The Medici family in Florence, Italy, brought together sculptors, scientists, poets, philosophers, painters, and architects. These men spawned the Renaissance, one of the most innovative eras in history.

Thirdly, innovators are consummate questioners. They have a passion for inquiry. They like to ask, "If we tried this, what would happen?"

Fourth, networking is key. This involves spending a lot of time with those who have diverse or conflicting ideas, with people who have different backgrounds and perspectives.

Section I: The Birthplace of Ideas

Fifth, innovators experiment. They are constantly trying out new ideas and visiting places where ideas and concepts are different than usual.

Sixth, innovation takes courage. It takes courage to be wrong and admit it to your associates and competitors. Only by recognizing and admitting your mistakes can you put them behind you and proceed with better ways to achieve your goals. The conclusions from this brief review might be: act different, think different, make a difference.

MATHEMATICS IS REALITY

Why does math work? Was it created or discovered? Over the years, asking questions has always, or almost always, been an interesting way to arrive at new ideas, although occasionally it fails to provide satisfactory answers. This is certainly true of the introductory questions for this section. I have occasionally pondered these questions, although it has never before led to a satisfactory answer.

A recent article by Mario Livio, an astrophysicist, provides some interesting material to think about but to my way of thinking does not fully answer the question. When we think about simple arithmetic, such as what 4 plus 4 equals, the answer is simple. It's one of life's certainties. Albert Einstein claimed it fits reality with such certainty that although primitive man probably discovered mathematics, it is as real as anything in our universe. Actually, when applied to physics or astronomy it is as useful as it is in calculating the proper change when you buy groceries. In fact, mathematical laws govern our cosmos. An atom twelve billion light-years away behaves just like an atom here on earth. Atoms behave according to mathematical laws that we have discovered, not created.

The formula for calculating the surface of a sphere remains just as correct as when Archimedes proved it around 250 BC, and the calculus described by Isaac Newton to describe motion is taught in high school and used by scientists all over the world.

The question as to whether mathematics was invented or discovered seems easy to answer. It was discovered as soon as humans began to adjust to the world around them. As our brains evolved, so did our understanding of mathematics. Fortunately, the better we understand, the more useful it becomes.

XENOPHILIA

Xenophon (430–554 BC) was unknown to me until recently when I read an article by Joseph Epstein. Xenophon was a student of Socrates but, because Plato's account of Socratic teaching has so dominated our literature, few of us have read Xenophon's extensive writings. Cicero stated the writings of Xenophon were extremely informative and extensive. It has been said that Plato's stories about Socrates are more Plato than Socrates, while Xenophon's stories concentrate more on Socrates' good sense, prudence, and order and are more practical. For those interested in Greek history, read a new book by

Section I: The Birthplace of Ideas

Robert Strassler who translated the ancient Greek manuscripts, concentrating on the Peloponnesian War. He was half-historian, half-philosopher, and a prolific and marvelous writer.

THE NEED TO CATEGORIZE

Ideas come from unexpected places. We have expected that they mostly come from people who are profound thinkers or from accidental incidents that bring a new idea to awareness for those intelligent enough to appreciate unconventional concepts. My twenty-five-year-old granddaughter, Stephanie, who has already demonstrated her ability to appreciate unconventional concepts she emphasizes in scientific writing, forwarded this idea to me.

It turns out that our brains are bombarded with so much information that we have need to sort it into categories to be able to use it effectively. This is not only true of people and animals, but probably primitive life forms. When we stop to think about it, we categorize almost everything: other people, animals, buildings, art, scientific data, plants, books, and ideas. If we consider how powerful this trait is, it will help us understand many things that may otherwise seem like somewhat of a mystery. Probably very nourishing food for thought.

SCIENCE AND PHILOSOPHY

Science tries to describe what happens and philosophy attempts to explain why things happen. Two of the most famous men in history to explain both of these concepts were Plato and Aristotle. The latter worked for twenty years in the Academy of Plato. The modern world owes much of the traditions of speculation, its criticism, and its deductive and inductive sciences to these ancient towers of intellect. Although they gave us a running start, it took several thousand years before their concepts were used to bring us to our present stage of understanding. The human need for god-like leaders and natural enemies generated the popularity of the various religious beliefs, heroes, and villains that, until a few generations ago, dominated our culture.

During the medieval epoch in Europe, theologians were the chief leaders in respect to dogmatic finality, but in the last three centuries the leadership in thought has largely been found in men of science, at least in the Western world. However, this leadership has only partly been accepted in many modern societies, probably due to a genetic need for approval from our peers.

It is interesting that Plato described Eros, meaning love, which he claimed would result in creative functions that would eventually lead to a state of human perfection. He also described the confusion and disorder in nature, which led him to deny the possibility of a supreme craftsman, a belief that has probably caused more conflict, murder, and misunderstanding than any belief held by society in the history of man.

Alfred Whitehead sums this up in his book *Adventures of Ideas* by listing the characteristics of an ideal civilization. He

Section I: The Birthplace of Ideas

claimed the five qualities are truth, beauty, adventure, art, and peace. In the last quality of peace he was not referring to political relations. He was referring to a quality of mind that has accepted the facts and environment he has become part of—a resignation, as it were, to the present life. Of course, this was written long before innovators became popular. They undoubtedly would have difficulty with his concepts.

HISTORICAL BELIEF SYSTEMS

Can slavery, unquestioning religious faith, aristocratic government, and disregard for the suffering of others pay off? In the Middle Ages they produced great cathedrals, beautiful palaces, and beautiful art. It may be that our belief in freedom, democracy, and human equality will make these icons of past civilization unattainable. This is the trade-off we must consider.

Yet we are better at adapting nature to human needs than ever before. These concepts of course are not new. Think of the fantastic aqueducts created by ancient Roman civilization, their great art, and the cultural centers such as Rome and Florence that at one time were the richest cities in Europe. Then, of course, there is Angkor Wat in Cambodia, an advanced civilization that was completely abandoned and later rediscovered, overgrown by jungle.

No matter how much we appreciate our present culture, we can probably learn a lot by studying those that went before. Would it be possible to design a new culture that would contain the advantages of the best of history and the best of our technology today? It seems unlikely. So few people learn about or appreciate what was best about the past.

John Armstrong, a modern philosopher, believes that an ideal civilization is material prosperity plus something else. The something else he claims is due to our acceptance of the appreciation of beauty, the quality of thought and feeling. Buddha claimed, *"The good life depends on complete detachment from worldly desires."* There is little chance this will be accepted in our present culture.

Today, things that are sensitive, tender, and beautiful seem to be vulnerable in our society. But I believe these are all compatible with today's culture. I have known many people who practice these traits and succeed also in business and the professions. These are ideas we must promote and practice to the best of our ability. If we do, we can look back with satisfaction. Maybe we can set an example for others. Maybe we can make a difference.

CONFUCIOUS FROM THE HEART BY YU DAN

This book, a best seller in China, was translated by a Chinese scholar in Britain, Esther Tyldesley. Highlights include:

- People who have only ambition and no realism are dreamers. Those who have only earth and no sky are only plodders, not realists.

Section I: The Birthplace of Ideas

- Confucius' attitude was extremely placid, yet his inner heart was very serious. His deep strength was rooted in his convictions.

- If you wish to raise yourself up, think of how to help other people raise themselves up.

- He constantly describes those he called Junze. A Junzi is described as a scholar and philosopher, the most desirable citizen. These people are described as having a steady sense of inner calm and an unhurried bearing. A Junzi has no worries or fears. When he reflects on his own conduct, he cannot find anything to regret or be ashamed of. To my mind this is an ideal that no realist could attain.

- Confucius said a gentleman agrees without being an echo. A small man echoes without being in agreement.

- He believed in stages of life. At thirty one should be able to take a stand by acquiring a bright, unhurried introspection that provides the ability to deal confidently and decisively with your own affairs.

- By this time Junzi should understand the yearning of their own spirit so as to make great plans or form great ambitions.

Yo Dan, the Chinese author of this book, from Beijing University, has sold ten million copies in China, even though it failed to mention modern Chinese communism.

Section II
Ideas Throughout History
(Medical Breakthroughs)

WILLIAM HARVEY

In the early sixteenth century, it was still widely believed according to the teachings of Galen, 300 years earlier, that blood sloshed back and forth through the circulation rather than circulated through the body. Harvey, a precocious student from England, went to medical school in Padua, Italy, then one of the foremost schools in Europe. While there, he met many original thinkers, including Galen, who was later arrested by the Catholic Church for claiming the earth circulated around the sun.

Harvey returned to London to practice but, because of his experience dissecting animals in Padua, was beginning to question Galen's teachings. After several years of

A Romance with Ideas

experiments, he was convinced that blood circulated due to the pumping of the heart, but he did not know how it got through the lungs. The pulmonary capillaries had not yet been discovered. He was reluctant to go public with his belief for many years but finally published his classic little book in 1628, "*du Motu Cordis,*" claiming the blood circulated and he gave evidence to support this. As he suspected, he was wildly criticized for several years, but as more people began to recognize that he was correct, eventually he was appointed physician to the king.

When we contemplate the medical progress that resulted from Harvey's idea that the blood circulated around and around and was propelled by the contractions of the heart muscle, it is mindboggling. Just think, he overturned the previous dogma that had dominated medical thinking for thousands of years. In a little more than four or five generations, knowledge rapidly increased until the specialty of cardiology is within reach of almost eradicating the death and disability of the number one cause of illness in the Western world. Although patients over sixty-five with cardiovascular disease are the most common reasons for hospitalization, the death and disability from cardiovascular disease has dramatically decreased in my lifetime. Not just in the aged, but most children born with abnormal hearts (congenital defects) are now being treated successfully, usually resulting in normal or near normal function. Harvey's ideas led to treatments that have saved millions of lives.

THE STETHOSCOPE

In 1816 it was known that when placing the ear to the chest one could hear a heart murmur. It had already been recognized that this identified defects in cardiac function. At the time all physicians were men, and placing the ear to the chest of a young woman was socially unacceptable.

Laennec, a young French physician suffering with chronic pulmonary tuberculosis, decided to roll up a quire of paper into a cylinder and place it on the chest of a young woman with severe heart disease. Why he did this was never explained. *"Much to my surprise, I could hear the heart sounds better than with my ear on the skin."* Over the years he modified the tube to produce the instrument that became the symbol of medicine—the stethoscope.

Henry Bourditch, an American doctor studying in Paris, published a book called *The Young Stethoscopist* that introduced the stethoscope to American medicine. He learned about this new instrument from Pierre Louis, said to be the best man in Paris with the device. Louis had been a friend and colleague of Laennec and had helped him make some modifications in the device before he died. Laennec died only a few years after he introduced the groundbreaking device that made him famous.

HEART CATHETERIZATION

Werner Forssman graduated from a German medical school in 1922 and began to believe that medicine injected directly into the heart would be beneficial. While training to be a surgeon in 1929, he convinced the chief surgical nurse, Frida Ditzen, to help him pass a urinary catheter from an arm vein into the heart. She volunteered to be the subject, but at the last moment he decided to do it on himself. With Frida's help, he did a cut down on a vein in his arm, passed a urinary catheter, and then went upstairs to the X-ray department and documented that it was in the right ventricle of the heart chamber that pumps blood to the lung. A few weeks later he passed a catheter into a terminally ill woman and, when she died, the autopsy confirmed its location, again in the right heart ventricle. He then repeated this on himself several times and then on dogs and rabbits, using thorotrast, a dye that can be imaged by X-ray, to document the location by X-ray.

When he reported what he had done at a surgical conference, the chief of surgery, Sauerbruch, was outraged and discharged him from the program. Twenty years later, after hearing about Forssman's experiences in 1951, Cournand, a pulmonary researcher, used the method to study blood pressure in the lungs. In 1956, Forssman, with Cournand and Richards, Cournand's assistant, received the Nobel Prize. Thus, heart catheterization was born, the procedure that advanced cardiology from then on by allowing doctors to diagnose problems in the heart. The procedure even today characterizes the specialty.

The heart is catheterized by passing a tube into the heart, either from a vein in the arm or in the groin. When this is advanced into the heart, the pressure in any chamber can be measured. Also, the concentration of oxygen in the blood can be measured or a dye can be injected through the catheter, which can be recorded on film. The location of the catheter is viewed using a fluoroscope.

Over the years cardiologists have learned to use this information to diagnose almost any abnormality, including obstructions in the coronary arteries, the pipelines that nourish the heart. Also diagnosed is disease in the heart valves or abnormalities in the chamber, the ventricle that indicates that the heart is failing to pump with adequate force, which leads to heart failure. This is usually accomplished with only a local anesthetic.

CORONARY ANGIOGRAPHY—MASON SONES

In 1958, in Cleveland Clinic, Mason Sones performed an aortagram by injecting a contrast agent just above the aortic valve in a twenty-five-year-old man with congenital heart disease. It had been established that the contrast agent was toxic to the heart when introduced in the coronary arteries but could be injected safely into the aorta, the large artery leaving the heart, to evaluate valve function. When the pressure injector containing dye was activated, the catheter accidentally migrated from aorta into the right coronary artery. As soon as the 40 mg of contrast agent entered the coronary artery, the patient's heart stopped. Sones shouted at the patient to cough, which, after a time, resulted in the heart restarting with a normal rhythm being reestablished.

Most physicians would have decided to never let that happen again. Not Mason Sones. When he examined the films that clearly showed the coronary arteries, which had been recorded with the injection, he realized here was a way to study coronary disease, the most common heart ailment in the world. After a time, he found that a smaller dose of contrast could be injected safely and soon developed the procedure of coronary angiography. This revolutionized cardiology and became one of the most common cardiac procedures in the Western world.

This experiment stimulated an Argentine doctor, Rene Favolaro, who worked in an animal lab at the Cleveland Clinic next to the catheterization lab, to develop the technique of using a vein graft excised from the patient's leg to *bypass* the obstructions in the coronary arteries. This operation has rehabilitated thousands of patients with anginal chest pain due to narrowed coronary arteries and probably prevented thousands of heart attacks. These two men with unconventional ideas changed cardiology forever.

A couple of years after he reported his experiences I traveled to Cleveland and learned the technique from Sones and formed a lifelong friendship with both Sones and Favolaro.

AFTERLOAD REDUCTION IN HEART FAILURE

In the early 1950s it was common for a patient with hypertension to arrive in the emergency room of Seaside Hospital in Long Beach, California, with acute pulmonary edema. These patients were struggling to breathe. Their lungs were full of fluid; they were cyanotic, the medical term for blue skin, indicating they were not getting enough oxygen, yet they were not surprisingly very frightened. This is a severe form of heart failure.

The common treatment was to use rotating tourniquets to reduce venous blood from returning to the lungs. They were also placed in oxygen tents and treated with morphine to relieve anxiety. Recovery, if it occurred, took several anxious hours.

As a young physician, I took my turn covering the emergency room, as was expected of newcomers, and worked with these patients. The results were not very satisfactory. They all had severe high blood pressure, and I reasoned that this was a burden on the weakened heart. At about this time, a new drug, hexamethonium, was released, which was reported to dramatically lower the blood pressure when injected intravenously. One evening, when treating a seventy-year-old hypertensive woman with severe pulmonary edema, it seemed to me she was not getting better in spite of our rotating tourniquets and oxygen tent. I decided to try this new drug to see if reducing her blood pressure would help. A small injection intravenously reduced her systolic pressure from 230 to 120 millimeters of mercury in only a few minutes. I was very worried that I might be making things worse, but within ten or fifteen minutes she was already breathing much easier. Her lungs sounded better and within thirty minutes she had lost her cyanosis and was much relieved. Needless to say, we were both elated.

From that day on acute pulmonary edema in our emergency room was treated with what we called afterload reduction, which means that the workload on the failing heart was reduced because the afterload—i.e., the blood pressure—was reduced, with excellent results. After thirty cases I reported my results at a medical seminar at a UCLA program at Harbor Hospital in Torrance, California. At the end of my presentation the chief of medicine got up and commented, "Very interesting report. If anyone uses this treatment in this hospital they will be immediately discharged."

After presenting the new treatment at a national meeting in 1953, it was finally accepted and became standard treatment after several years.

CHRONOTROPIC INCOMPETENCE
(Medical Term for Slow Heart Rate)

Over the years it became established that people who were sedentary and had limited endurance had a rapid heart rate with exercise, and well-conditioned athletes had a much slower heart rate for any given exercise level. In the early days of maximum exercise testing at our hospital, we had many experiences to confirm this as we occasionally tested marathon runners, as well as sedentary "couch potatoes." (Maximum

Section II: Ideas Throughout History

exercise on a treadmill was used to diagnose obstructed coronary arteries that often led to heart attacks.)

In 1973, this new diagnostic procedure using the treadmill in order to diagnose coronary artery disease was becoming recognized locally, as well as nationally, when an unusual event occurred. A woman friend of my wife's asked me to do a test on her husband. He was fifty-four years old and had just sold his business and was planning an extensive vacation. He claimed he had no symptoms but agreed to have the exercise test to satisfy his wife because his father had died of a heart attack. He had been a college football star but said he had been sedentary over the last twenty years. He was tested on the treadmill to his maximum capacity and did not have chest pain or signs of problems on his electrocardiogram or blood pressure, but he had one curious finding. His heart rate during exercise was far below average for his age. When quizzed about this, he denied any recent physical training, claiming he had been sedentary for years. He was advised the test was normal and a week later they left for Tahiti. A week after they left town I received a call from his distraught wife. While swimming in the surf he had dropped dead. His wife had his body brought home and an autopsy revealed severe coronary artery disease. How did we not diagnose it with the stress test? We believed this newly developed exercise test was a reliable way to detect coronary artery disease. The only abnormality was the curiously slow heart rate. Yet he had assured us he had done nothing to be well-conditioned and had not experienced any chest pain, often a sign of coronary heart disease.

Fortunately, we were in the late stages of a study on 2,000 treadmill tests using maximum stress, a new concept. (Maximum stress was identified when the patient was unable to exercise further). All the data had been entered in our new CDC mainframe computer, including data we had entered on their heart rate during the test and the follow-up. This included heart attacks, mortality, and so on.

A review of the heart rate response and the follow-up of the patients revealed that among other patients with a slow heart rate even though they exercised to capacity during the test, the mortality rate was very high. A surprising discovery since we had been convinced that a slow heart rate response to exercise was a sign of excellent health. So, we named this response "chronotropic incompetence," a medical term for a slow heart rate response to maximum exercise. It was a new concept. Subsequent research has confirmed our findings over and over.

Another example of serendipity?

PACEMAKERS

As a teenager, Wilson Greatbatch, a ham radio enthusiast with a love of gadgets, worked on the Cornell Animal Farm to help measure brain waves. He discussed this work with a couple of surgeons who mentioned that abnormal cardiac rhythms were often dangerous. Years later, while teaching engineering, he was helping to design a better device to record the heartbeat of animals and, accidentally, his device started stimulating the animal's heart at an increased heart rate.

Abnormal heart rhythms were studied for many years by the innovative electrocardiogram developed by the Dutch physician, Einthoven, in 1860. But when the heart rate got too slow, nothing could be done. However, Greatbatch had spent several years experimenting with a device in dogs and finally, in 1960, implanted it in patients. Thus, this unplanned event in animals led the way to treat heart block, a common condition resulting in a very slow heart rate. Greatbach attributed his breakthrough to errors he had made experimenting with electronics. Many times mistakes such as the one made by Greatbatch and by Mason Sones, when he accidentally injected dye into the coronary artery, lead to a new way of thinking and a new way to manage problems.

The early battery-powered pacemakers were used to treat patients with heart block. This is a condition where the normal electrical circuit that sends the electrical stimulus from the upper chamber, the atrium, to the lower chamber, the ventricle, is interrupted for some reason. The ventricle responds by initiating a heart rate of between twenty to thirty beats per minute. Thus, the heart's pumping capacity is dramatically reduced. At this slow rate it will usually sustain life, but patients are severely limited and are unable to exercise and often develop heart failure, with fluid accumulating in their lungs and edema in their feet and legs. These first pacemakers had a fixed heart rate, usually about seventy beats per minute, were quite large, producing a large bulge under the skin where they were implanted, and they had a short battery life, usually about one year. When the battery gave out a new one would have to be implanted at another surgery.

In the last few years pacemakers have been miniaturized, their rate can be set at any desirable level, their lithium batteries can last as long as seven or eight years, and they can store the electrocardiogram, which can be viewed with appropriate equipment. This is an example where the marvels of electronics, coupled with innovative people such as Greatbatch, have provided the means to return patients to normal health during the last fifty years.

SMALLPOX—EDWARD JENNER

Lady Montague, wife of the British ambassador to the Ottoman Empire, who was recognized for her beauty and style, contracted smallpox in 1784. About 30% of those who were infected died in the 1800s. Even though the pox left Lady Montague disfigured, she accompanied her husband to Turkey where it was a common practice to inoculate people with the materials from pustules. It was believed to be safe, although it did not totally eliminate death from the pox. In

Section II: Ideas Throughout History

England, six weeks of bleeding, fasting, and purging was routinely prescribed prior to the treatment of Lady Montague. An example of how a non-physician with a personal interest introduced an idea from Turkey.

Because of Lady Montague's report, Edward Jenner, son of a clergyman who came from a small town, had been treated with the inoculation as a child. He aspired to become a physician but, because he had not completed elementary school, was unable to be admitted to a medical school. So, as was then the practice, he was apprenticed to a surgeon for six years. He met milkmaids who, because they had acquired cowpox, declared they were immune to smallpox. He also became friendly with John Hunter who was helping Captain Cook catalog specimens from his South Pacific voyages. This led Jenner to be interested in many medical conditions and non-medical science. His recognition that the "weaker pox," cowpox, gave protection, and his familiarity with the story of Lady Montague and his treatment led him to inoculate his son with swinepox, followed by also injecting his gardener. When he tried to report his results to the Royal Society in 1797, it was rejected so he published it in a private pamphlet. Thus he established the concept that was described by Lady Montague years before.

Although this type of uncontrolled experiment is no longer condoned, it points out that trial and error has been used in science for hundreds of years. Almost all discoveries came from trial and error before research became institutionalized in the nineteenth century. Formalized research is relatively new. We should recognize that this methodology still has utility in our understanding of the world.

Other Breakthrough Ideas that Changed the World

THE EARTH ROTATES AROUND THE SUN

Nicholas Copernicus first published the Heliocentric Theory in a little pamphlet in 1514. He was not an astronomer. He was Polish by birth and an undistinguished church administrator who studied at Krakow University and believed in a harmonic, mathematically-structured universe. He searched for order and was interested in keeping the calendar accurate. He figured out that by placing the sun in the center and designated circular orbits it was more useful in predicting events. Most astronomers agreed and considered his ideas an improved way to calculate planetary positions, not a description of how the universe really is. He dedicated his article to the Pope, but it was unlikely that the Pope or any of his important advisors read it. Thus, an obscure article by an unimportant Polish mathematician failed to create an uproar.

Unlike Copernicus, Galileo was an astronomer for the court of the Medici family and because of their influence, he generated a lot of attention. He named some of the planets

Section II: Ideas Throughout History

he discovered to honor his sponsors and made flamboyant speeches describing his belief that the sun was the center of the universe. Galileo also reported that the wine, believed to be transformed into the blood of Christ by the priests, could not be true. Around this time, millions of Europeans were now reading due to Gutenberg's printing press. The church felt threatened and in 1641 forced Galileo to disavow his claims and placed him on house arrest for the rest of his life. Christians were advised that they could not read his articles.

THE PRINTING PRESS—GUTENBERG

In about 1440, Johannes Gutenberg, who lived in the Rhineland, the center of the wine industry in Germany, began tinkering with a wine press. These presses had been used for generations to make wine, but Gutenberg was not interested in wine. He knew the Chinese had used a press to reproduce art for centuries, which was introduced by a blacksmith named P. Sheng. Gutenberg had been trained as a goldsmith and had learned how to imprint things on lead. Combining this with the vintners' press, he was able to print multiple copies of the Bible. This invention turned millions of illiterate Europeans into readers for the first time. Although it has been reported that Gutenberg himself only printed 180 copies, his methodology was quickly picked up by others, which introduced the Bible to countless people.

Steven Johnson claimed this type of borrowing is called exaptation, a word coined by brilliant scientist Stephen J. Gould in 1971. Gutenberg claimed, "I took a machine designed to get people drunk and turned it into an engine for mass communication."

The impact the printing press had on society is so important it can hardly be measured. All at once people all over the world began to appreciate and be aware of how people in other societies were living, thinking, and relating to people next door and in far-off lands. The differences in religion and the ideas and innovations of people all over the world could be evaluated, discussed, and experimented with.

Anthropologists believe that the reason the human brain has outstripped other large-brained animals is because we learned how to communicate. The printing press increased our ability to communicate and is believed to be one of the most important inventions in our culture. It may be an important reason why progress keeps accelerating in recent history.

EVOLUTION

Charles Darwin, who changed the world of science with his description of evolution, was a very unusual young man, even before his three-year trip on the sailing ship *Beagle* to explore the Southern Hemisphere. Although his father, a physician, and his uncle, Erasmus Darwin, had decided he should be a preacher, as a young man he had always been a voracious reader. He was also an amateur naturalist who collected plants and primitive animals like snails and shellfish.

One of his professors, Henslow, who turned down the trip that Darwin made, recommended Charles in his place. He remarked, "Charles has a brain that sops up knowledge like litmus paper, and also for coming up with speculative theories," a statement that later was confirmed by events. Although at first his family was against his making the trip, his grandfather convinced the family he should go. Another professor, Charles Lyell, who observed seashells on mountaintops, and had just published his theories that the earth was millions of years old, had a strong influence on Darwin's reasoning. Darwin had accompanied Lyell on several field trips.

Modern authors have credited his observations on the Galapagos Islands with his final description of evolution. On the Galapagos he observed the shape of the beaks of finches and correlated this with their changing diet. His habit of keeping detailed notes of his observations and his thoughts about what he saw suggest that it was years after he observed these little birds that he conceived the idea that inherited traits changed life and the nature of animals over time. A review of his notebooks reveals that it was at least ten years later, after he had returned to England in 1830, that he first formulated the theory of natural selection. It was almost twenty years after that, in 1859, when he finally went public following the receipt of a letter from Alfred Wallace in South America, who had arrived at the same conclusion. His book, which shook the world, *The Origin of the Species*, sold out the first day. However, of interest, today everyone in science believes his thesis, but over half of the American public rejects his ideas almost 100 years later.

Although his ideas were earthshaking, they were the result of numerous observations and probably many preliminary ideas, as well as the ability to combine many concepts into a coherent system. It is a skill that history has revealed is essential in discovery but is not too common.

Of interest, the man who noticed seashells on mountaintops and had a strong influence on Darwin, Lyell, published his book shortly after Darwin sailed on the *Beagle*. Lyell's book, *The Principles of Geology*, sold twelve editions. Lyell was convinced that mountains were once under the sea and had been erupting for millions of years, more evidence the earth was not made in seven days.

Soon after Darwin's book was published in 1860, a meeting of the British Association for the Advancement of Science, where Darwin's book was featured, attracted almost 1,000 people. Darwin's friend, Huxley, agreed to be the protagonist. The Bishop of Oxford, Samuel Coil, when he introduced Huxley asked him, "Do you claim kinship to apes from your grandfather or your grandmother?" Huxley retorted, "I would rather claim kinship with an ape than to someone who used his eminence to propose such uninformed twaddle into what was supposed to be a serious scientific forum." The crowd responded with an uproar.

Section II: Ideas Throughout History

Some claimed Darwin had rewritten the *Book of Genesis*. In the last 100 years, Darwin's theory has been validated over and over and is accepted by almost all scientists. Darwin died in 1882 and was buried in Westminster Abbey, next to Isaac Newton.

ALTERNATIVE VIEWS ON EVOLUTON

Although Darwin is famous and admired by most scientists, there are many intellectuals, not just religious types, that disagree with some of his ideas.

Darwin proposed that evolution was due to accidental errors in DNA, resulting in offspring that were better suited to the environment. This leaves us with some difficult issues that should be considered.

At the beginning of the nineteenth century Lamarck wrote a book, *Philoshie Zoologique*, that claimed acquired characteristics could be passed on and inherited by our offspring. He claimed that evolution is a cumulative process whereby the efforts and achievements of individuals would be passed on, thus improving the family tree.

This idea conflicts with Darwin's thesis, but Lamarck's ideas were well established before Darwin's book, *The Origin of the Species*, was published in 1859.

Thus, it would appear that the two concepts might be incompatible, but maybe they both are taking place simultaneously.

A Romance with Ideas

In 1970 the magazine *The New Scientist* published an article, "The Big Reverse for the Dogma of Biology." The implication was that a new study established that Darwin's theory was wrong. They reported on a research paper that in certain bacteria external agents could alter the hereditary blueprint, which could be beneficial or harmful. Thus, the conclusion was that Lamarck's claim that environmental influences could create changes in the genetic substrate was proven.

Arthur Koestler, a prolific author, claims in his book, *Janus: A Summing Up*, "that besides natural selection, purposeful behavior is inherent in our nature and is important in evolution." Lamarck believed these changes were gradual and took many generations to be manifested. Koestler questions, "How can the birds' ability to build elaborate nests or spiders to weave beautiful webs be explained except by recognizing that they come from learned abilities, passed on from ancestors for generations?" Koestler points out that Darwin himself acknowledged this in his last book, *The Variation of Plants and Animals Under Domestication*.

Albert Szent-Gyorgyi, a Nobel Laureate, coined the term "syntropy" as counter to entropy to describe the innate drive of living matter to protect itself. He also agreed that creatures, over time, had the capacity to build complex structures out of simpler elements. It would appear that besides natural selection, purposeful behavior is inherent in life and probably alters the course of history.

Section II: Ideas Throughout History

Koestler claims, "Evolution is like a journey from an unknown origin, to an unknown destination. We sail along a vast ocean, but we can at least chart the route which has carried us from the sea-cucumber state to the conquest of the moon." Koestler points out that the rapid growth of the brain in primitive man developed far in advance of the needs of its possessor. It has taken man thousands of years to learn how to use it. Are we there yet?

GENETICS—GREGOR MENDEL

Gregor Mendel, the son of a farmer, was born in 1822 in Heinzendorf, Austria, today Hynice, Czechoslovakia. His father had served as a soldier for eight years and then came home to operate his grandfather's farm. Gregor's mother, Rosine, was the daughter of the village gardener, who taught Mendel about growing things. He also learned about the family fruit orchards.

During his elementary education he demonstrated exceptional academic ability. He enrolled in Olmutz University and tried to pay his expenses by tutoring students. His sister donated her dowry to send him there, where he learned physics and mathematics and was supported by one of his professors, Frederick Franz, who recommended he go to the Altbrunn Monastery where he was assigned to care for their large herbarium and botanical garden. After a short while he was recommended for priesthood and shortly after, a sub-deacon and a priest. While at the monastery he became a substitute teacher part time.

He also became a member of the Brunn Horticultural Society. During this time he worked in the monastery garden and kept careful records of how yellow and green peas reproduced. He demonstrated that parental traits do not blend but would always reproduce yellow or green in predictable ratios.

He read a paper describing his findings before the Natural History Society of Brunn and it was published in their proceedings in 1865, and a copy of his paper was sent to the Swiss botanist, Kare-Wilhelm-Nagali, who failed to perceive its importance, even though Mendel presented his results in precise mathematical formulae. His results weren't quite as widely ignored as some believed since they were described in the *Encyclopedia Britannica* and quoted by several recognized scientists of the day.

This went unnoticed by Darwin, however, who published his *Origin of the Species* a few years before in 1859. Finally Mendel's experiments were repeated in the early twentieth century. Thus, the first geneticist was only recognized after DNA and chromosomes were described 100 years later. He was forty-four years old when he presented his results at the Society of Brunn. In about 1880 he developed renal insufficiency and died at the age of sixty-two. He only became world famous after his work was repeated almost 100 years later.

BRAILLE

Louis Braille, a fifteen-year-old blind boy, invented the tactile form of reading that revolutionized the life of the blind in 1821. He was familiar with a rudimentary system called "bump," a tactile text invented by an army captain, Charles Barbier, and revised it to become the tactile text that is still in use today. For almost 200 years no one has come up with a better way for the blind to read. This is a remarkable tribute to a teenage boy and emphasizes that innovation can come from almost anywhere. This remarkable achievement, a system that makes it possible for the blind to understand life, was the work of a fifteen-year-old who, before his invention, was relatively uneducated.

DYNAMITE

In 1863, Alfred Nobel experimented with nitroglycerine and developed a way to detonate it. He named it dynamite. This not only made him millions of dollars but also revolutionized war and construction work. We now know about his prizes that reward innovative ideas in science and occasionally even in government. Nobel recognized that his invention would result in a more destructive way to make war and that his foundation to reward those who excelled in science would stimulate progress and balance the destructive nature of his invention.

A Romance with Ideas

SPUTNIK

On October 7, 1957, the Soviets launched *Sputnik*, the first man made orbiting satellite that startled the world. Two young physicists at Johns Hopkins University, William Guier and George Wiffenbach, excitedly discussed what kind of microwave signal might be detectible. They were both in a PhD program on microwave spectroscopy. That afternoon they found they could pick up the signal of *Sputnik* and could estimate its orbit and position.

A year later Guier and Wiffenbach were asked by Frank McClure, the director of the applied physics lab, "Can you reverse the calculations and, if you know the orbit, could you locate the receiver on the ground?" After some number crunching the answer was yes. This was then used by the military to locate submarines from orbiting satellites.

Today, our satellites allow us to locate everything with the GPS. There is no reason to get lost. Navigating on the ocean has been revolutionized as well as finding almost anything. GPS, the system that has evolved from the curiosity of Guier and Wiffenbach, is responsible for the maps your computer makes, and for the concern that anyone with a cell phone can be located without their knowledge. The erosion of our privacy has been an unexpected side effect of the curiosity of a couple of very smart men.

Comment: There are several hundred similar stories that could be told. The important point is that none of these

Section II: Ideas Throughout History

breakthroughs came from planned, sponsored research. There were no research grants involved, no research councils, and rarely university PhDs involved, with the exception of the *Sputnik* story. An outstanding cardiologist from Texas claimed, "Great discoveries in medicine are rarely made by panels of experts." This has been called gang or group approach. Great discoveries originate in the minds of single individuals. You can hire men but not ideas. However, their discoveries are usually due to an innovative person who has many ideas that lead to a breakthrough.

These scientific breakthroughs came from inquisitive people, usually from those who knew quite a lot about a lot of things. But they not only knew a lot, they were able to combine several facts into a concept that provided a new way of thinking, of making sense out of something previously recognized. Someone once said that innovation occurs when you look at something everyone has seen but you think it has a different meaning or utility.

SUPERCONDUCTIVITY

In April 1911 physicist Heike Kammerlingh Onnes scrawled in his notebook, "Mercury practically 0." Actually, he and his team at Laden University in the Netherlands had cooled a sample of mercury to within 3 degrees of absolute 0 and recorded that electrical resistance vanished. They had discovered *superconductivity*.

Since then, the theory of superconductivity has been applied to nuclear matter, liquid helium, and atomic gases.

The reason for this fact stumped brilliant scientists such as Werner Heisenberg, Albert Einstein, and Richard Feynman. Finally, Leon Cooper, a graduate student at the University of Illinois, showed that superconductivity arises when electrons in metal form pairs that cannot be deflected without severing their bonds, requiring energy unavailable at low temperatures. This produced a Nobel Prize for Cooper and his co-investigators in 1986. This led to the understanding of several events in astronomy such as what holds neutron stars together.

BELIEF AND THE BRAIN

Psychological studies support the concept that understanding or comprehension of a statement entails the tacit acceptance of its being true, whereas disbelief required a more comprehensive process of rejection. That is, we need to analyze an idea in more detail to bring ourselves to reject it. Spinoza claimed belief comes quickly and naturally, while skepticism is slow or unnatural.

Most of our institutions, religion, politics, and economics reward belief in the doctrines of faith or party ideology and punish those who challenge authority and discourage uncertainty and skepticism. Thus, it is easier to convince people of some positive issue than that of a negative one.

Section II: Ideas Throughout History

There are a number of examples of beliefs that are popular, although common sense should tell us otherwise. These include UFOs, mind reading, astrology, and ghosts. The evidence that there is no science to support these concepts as well as many other beliefs is no deterrent to millions of people. There are many belief systems that make us feel good, thus they are accepted on flimsy evidence, usually because we wish them to be true or because our friends claim them to be true.

One of the best books discussing the reasons for these beliefs is by Michael Shermer, *The Believing Brain*. For those who would like to study this process, I recommend it. He concludes that the brain is a belief engine. It looks for and finds patterns and then infuses them with meaning, forming beliefs. It is common that two very intelligent people examine the same material and arrive at diametrically opposite opinions. These are based on our culture, belief systems, and factors that we are emotionally comfortable with. It seems unlikely this will ever change.

THE IDEA OF DEMOCRACY

Although it had been practiced in a limited way in ancient Rome, the idea that there were private rights that lay absolutely beyond the jurisdiction of the government and the people themselves was a remarkable innovation. American democracy was a radical idea and one of the most important events in modern history.

A Romance with Ideas

The idea that sovereignty could be located outside the government was totally new. The U.S. Constitution was designed to protect the public from the government, from our leaders, as well as from certain elements of the private sector, and it had never been tried before.

An important contributor to this document was George Mason, considered the father of the Bill of Rights. He was from the state of Virginia and was one of the most influential representatives at the Constitutional Convention. Now, almost 300 years later, almost half of the governments on earth have instituted a democracy somewhat patterned on the one created by our founders. James T. Banner recently quoted Gordon Wood who wrote in 1776, "When the Constitution was being drafted, when society is disordered, and when questions come faster than answers, ideas become truly vital and creative."

The major weaknesses of our representative government have turned out to be that when large segments of society become non-contributors, they vote to confiscate the wealth of those who are contributing. Margaret Thatcher remarked, "The problem is we eventually run out of other people's money." This has happened in Greece today and is also complicated by the tendency for government to constantly expand and stifle the efforts of productive citizens with more and more regulations.

In spite of our democracy's faults, it has resulted in a unique civilization that is the envy of most of the educated people of the world.

Section III
―◄o►―
Ideas Today

TECHONOMY—SOCIAL POWER

Over the last several hundred years technology, democracy, capitalism, and education have resulted in dramatic changes in our lifestyle and culture. Many of the details of this revolutionary process have been featured in this book.

In a recent issue of *Forbes* magazine—probably the Bible of most businessmen in the United States—an article featured the importance of information, not only to scientists and businesses but also to social changes throughout the world. The recent uprisings in Egypt, Tunisia, Libya, and Syria, the so-called Arab Spring, were probably in large part due to the explosion of information. When Gutenberg started printing the Bible, millions learned how to read. This facilitated dramatic progress as they learned what was happening to people everywhere. *Forbes* has labeled this trend "techonomy."

In the last few years the explosion of information has not only resulted in millions of people demanding a better life, but it has provided the opportunity for those who are working in American businesses to influence management like never before. David Kirkpatrick believes Facebook and Twitter have not only knocked down dictators in Arab countries but are dramatically changing the way we do business. He states, "Employees and customers will be calling the shots." Already management has begun to respond more to the demands of their employees and their customers.

Examples of this trend were reported from major companies from all over the Western world, from Australia and New Zealand to Sweden, Britain, and France, as well as the United States, where it is most prevalent. He claims, "The idea of a hierarchy that fundamentally empowers the few and disempowers the many is more or less dead." Observing this movement in the next few years will be fascinating. I would guess it may be a powerful social force.

SOCIALISM VS. CAPITALISM

Today, the political parties are lined up against each other in a deadly battle. Alfred North Whitehead, an acclaimed philosopher in 1932, claimed that big business is quite similar to slavery. He says individualists and socialists are debating over

Section III: Ideas Today

the details of neo-feudalism, which modern industry requires. He claimed the self-sufficient, independent man is a concept without any validity in modern civilization.

Whitehead pontificates, *"Thou shalt not murder,"* but tradition approves all sorts of competition tantamount to murder. The industrial system, which started in England, evolved into a system that he calls industrial slavery. He claims that this social trend was promoted by Darwin's belief in the survival of the fittest. He said these were the ideas that would lead to the demise of "Christian brotherhood."

I feel sure that Darwin would reject this reasoning. Darwin went on record, in fact, before he died rejecting the idea that survival of the fittest in business was in any way related to the genetic processes he described. His theory explained how life evolved over millions of years, not how economic forces became prominent.

Whitehead's beliefs have been disproved by history, of course. There has never been a socialist society that has been successful so far. As anyone who studied political history knows, socialistic governments have perpetrated misery and suffering wherever they have been instituted. A modern example is North Korea, while right next door capitalism in South Korea has produced one of the most successful societies in modern times. Capitalism provides a system where the fruits of innovation can be made available to almost everyone, thus providing a better life to all.

THE EVOLUTION OF SMARTS

It has been obvious for a long time that humans, with their large brains, are smarter than any other animal. How we got that way and what will happen in the future is and has been under intense study for years. Although our large brain size is one factor, some large animals, like elephants, whales, and porpoises, have a larger brain but are obviously not as smart. The reasons for this are still unclear, but our ability to communicate has certainly been one factor. The printing press, radio, computer, and the Internet have all improved our reasoning. Are we near maximum capacity? An analysis of the intellect of great minds—such as Michelangelo, Albert Einstein, Socrates, Isaac Newton, and Charles Darwin—suggests, they were as smart as anyone alive today or in the recent past.

In one of his recent books, Steven Jay Gould states that humans will not improve physically or mentally in the future. He describes the near maximum performance in sports records recently. No one has exceeded or matched the batting averages of Ted Williams of 0.406 and Joe DiMaggio's 56-game hitting streaks. These are sporting events he believes are all-time maximums. The world records in other sporting events, such as the 100-yard dash, continue to improve, however. Maybe they are also near maximum. Only time will tell. Gould also believes that there will never be another composer like Wagner and that the brilliant, innovative people in modern science and business have gone about as far as they can go.

Section III: Ideas Today

A recent article in the *Scientific American* by Simon Laughlin of Cambridge University claims our cortical gray matter neurons are working with axons pretty close to the limit. Although this may be true, brilliant minds are bouncing ideas off each other at unprecedented frequency, which may contribute to the advance of civilization's knowledge base for a long time.

THE CURSE OF ADMINISTRATION

Although most of us acknowledge the need for administration, there seems to be a consensus that at least in business, science departments, hospitals, and other complex organizations, administrators rarely fully understand what brings the highest quality to the product and the most satisfaction to the workers. In the institutions where I have worked it is rare for administrators to spend much time in areas where the work is performed. It is rare that they are trained or have practiced the skills of those in the work force. At the Cleveland Clinic, one of the outstanding medical centers in the Western world, they have always had a physician as the head administrator. Their success should have sent a message, but hospitals have not listened.

Administrators usually try to convince everyone that their way is best, despite rejection by those in the trenches, or even their customers. Their ideas, of course, usually prevail because they hold the power of the purse. This often results in the loss of some of their most productive staff, thus reducing the chance for progress and overall success. This has certainly been the case where I have worked.

The chief of General Electric, one of the most successful corporations in the world, once stated, *"I spend at least one-third of my time wandering around. I need to hear what those in production, in research, are thinking and doing."* What a shining example of what a successful administrator should be doing. Yet, this is a rare event in the businesses of America. Still, administration keeps expanding. A recent article reported that U.C. Davis, one of California's state-supported colleges, now has more administrators than teachers. Hospitals now spend more than 25% of their budget on administration. This burden is expanding every day. Already recently-enacted ObamaCare is creating new administrative burdens.

A recently published book by Benjamin Ginsberg, *The Fall of the Faculty*, reports the number of administrators has increased dramatically in most schools in the last ten years—103% at Williams College, 111% at Johns Hopkins, 325% at Wake Forrest, to name just a few. He claims administration views research as a source of revenue rather than advancing knowledge. At most schools even mid-level administrators are paid more than faculty. A recent article in the *Orange County Register* reported that the Vice Chancellor for Medical Affairs at U.C. Irvine, a state-supported school, is paid $743,931 per year, the Dean of the Medical Schools $464,000, and the Chancellor $374,969.

Section III: Ideas Today

This parallels the enormous increase in government jobs that has not only resulted in a significant increase in the financial burden, but the regulations they introduce reduce the efficiency of our businesses and organizations. An example of this increase is from 1950 when I joined the staff of our hospital; I filled out a one-page form. Last year, in order to continue those privileges I filled out a 35-page form, requiring my signature on 16 of those pages. Where will it ever end?

THE CREDIT FOR DISCOVERIES

Over the years, scientists have strived to receive credit for their discoveries, usually by publishing articles in peer-reviewed journals. The story of the discovery of the Ice Age illustrated a common event, however.

A naturalist, Jean De Carpentier, said he was walking along a country lane with a Swiss woodcutter. He was remarking about the unusual rocks along the road and the woodcutter replied, *"They came from the Grimsel Glacier."* He told de Carpentier that the glacier *"at one time reached all the way to Bern."* Later, a discussion with a botanist named Karl Schimpter termed it the Ice Age (in German, Eiszeit) in 1837. Then a controversy developed as to who should be credited with the discovery of the Ice Age.

Agassiz, a professor in Switzerland, described three stages of discovery. First, they deny it is an important discovery, then claim it is true, and finally credit the wrong person. This is often the case. Should we credit the woodcutter or de

Carpentier, or the botanist Karl Schimpter, or does it matter who gets the credit?

THE PREVALENCE OF UNSCIENTIFIC BELIEFS

It is of interest that although science has become established as a way to answer many questions, create all types of inventions, and has become the backbone of the business and corporations in the Western world, much of the facts identified by science are rejected by more than half of Americans. One of the most unscientific beliefs that is popular in the United States is creationism. A number of organizations, including Creation Ministries International and Young Earth International, have branches in Australia, Canada, New Zealand, South Africa, and the United Kingdom, as well as the U.S. They bring in millions of dollars annually. Even the chief of our National Institute of Health, the premier governmental science agency, Francis Collins, is said to believe in creationism.

The synonym for creationism has recently become "intelligent design," which is now taught in many of our schools. The popularity of this belief is difficult for most scientists to understand, but this is probably due to the prejudices instilled in childhood that many find impossible to abandon.

THE BELIEF IN GOD TODAY

The Oxford University Press claims that 84% of the world's population belong to some form of organized religion. This

Section III: Ideas Today

equals 507 billion people. A Pell forum survey found the following percent of belief:

God or universal spirit 92%
Heaven 74%
Hell 59%
Miracles 79%

The belief that there must be something else out there is so common that 21% of atheists and 55% of agnostics believe in some sort of god or universal spirit.

Almost all primitive societies have rules about sharing, proposed by most religions, and most have some supernatural force or person who preaches this. Cultures with these beliefs prospered and thus their genes were passed on. Most people claim benevolence is also desirable and favored by their god or deity.

I believe humans create gods, not vice versa. Various gods like Amon Ra, Aphrodite, Apollo, Bael, Brahma, Ganesha, Isis, Mithra, Osiris, Shiva, Thor, Vishnu, Wotan, Zeus, and hundreds of others have held sway over the years. Are they all false gods? Depending on your culture you usually believe in the god that your friends believe in, the one that is predominant in your culture.

Virgin births produced Dionysis, Buddha, Krishna, Romulus, and of course Jesus. Resurrection myths were also common. In

Egypt it was Osiris. Shortly after Jesus was resurrected, another resurrection, Apollonius of Tyana, in Asia Minor occurred. There is no shortage of resurrections.

According to a Harris poll, the incidence of beliefs are as follows: God 82%, soul survival 71%, heaven 75%, hell 61%, and reincarnation 20%. This is quite similar to the Pell Survey. The afterlife is a type of idealism. Most people believe our minds are separate from our bodies.

Our brains are naturally inclined to weave all sensory inputs and cognitive thoughts into a meaningful story with ourselves as the central character. For those who believe in the afterlife, belief comes first, rational reasons for this come second. We will almost always find a way to believe or support what we want to believe.

How meaningful are our lives, our family, our friends, our communities, and how we treat others? The result does not serve as a prop to prepare for an eternal tomorrow where the ultimate purpose will be revealed to us, but a valued essence in the here and now. Recognizing this elevates us to a higher plane of humanity.

There is no doubt that a belief in God makes people feel better, especially in times of trouble. A recent funeral of a friend illustrated this effect. The majority of those in attendance were very senior. There was little doubt that the assurance that there was something good following death proposed by the preacher was a comfort to most of those in attendance.

HOW TO EXPLAIN THE BELIEF SYSTEMS OF EDUCATED PEOPLE

Over the years, as I continued to study and read about the different belief systems that people share, I have become more and more surprised. There was a time when I believed that belief systems held by various people were due to their intelligence. As time passed I realized that dramatically different belief systems were not due to peoples' lack of intelligence but due to their environment. Of course, one's environment is partly related to intelligence, but only in a small degree. It was obvious that many Catholics and Protestants were equally intelligent. Many Moslems and Jews were very intelligent and politically, conservatives and liberals are both intelligent.

When we examine these groups it becomes obvious that intelligence, or a lack thereof, does not help to understand this dilemma. So what might explain these differences?

The first thing that probably plays a most important role is environment. A person born and raised in a group that has a strong belief in a certain religion or some other culture is more likely to follow along with the beliefs of his peers. A wise man once said, *"Give me a child for the first 8 years and I will have him in my camp forever."* The truth of this can be confirmed by observing the power of belief systems still prevalent in the Moslem, Christian, Jewish, and Oriental societies.

The next most powerful influence is the society that people elect to affiliate with as they mature. Those who decide to become professors in our universities in America almost always affiliate with the liberal, democratic political system. Those who go into business are more likely to affiliate with a more conservative political system, obviously because it is more favorable to their economic livelihood, but also because it is most popular among their friends and associates.

George Cunningham, an MD and a geneticist, who was raised as a Catholic but began to have doubts about religion over the years, has developed some ideas about the belief in God and ended up writing a provocative book entitled *Decoding the Language of God*. His book was in response to a famous scientist, Francis Collins, MD, who is the Chief of the National Institute of Health, and a geneticist who is widely published. Dr. Collins recently published a book explaining why he believes in God even though over 90% of scientists are atheists. For those interested in this controversy, reading Cunningham's book is enlightening and very convincing. On the other hand, it does not explain all the reasons why he and Collins disagree or why diverse societal religious and political beliefs are so strongly held by otherwise intelligent people. I believe there are more people examining this issue now than in the past and probably more people who change their persuasion than ever before as populations mix geographically and culturally.

Michael Shermer, in his recent book *The Science of Good and Evil*, claims the mind is only capable of including certain

Section III: Ideas Today

preconceived ideas, and Phillip Howard in *The Death of Common Sense* doubts there is much hope for a logical answer. Only time will tell.

THE EVOLUTION OF IDEAS

An early English philosopher, Alfred Whitehead, had ideas almost 100 years ago worth reviewing. He had an enormous grasp of history and believed that religion and the advance of technology together were the driving force that moved society from one where slavery and the limited value of human life were replaced by our modern concepts of freedom and the importance of the individual. The concept of central control was replaced by competition. Although there is still a sizeable number of people who believe that this life is only a way to prepare for a perfect life in the hereafter, more and more are living as if heaven can be realized on earth. In fact, there is evidence that this attitude, a form of hedonism, if carried to the extreme could destroy many of the benefits our modern technology has bestowed upon us.

When we observe the belief systems that drive modern politics, it is often a reminder of the intense feelings that were the backbone of primitive societies. This inherited emotional need to segregate people according to "them versus us," and the inherited tribal feelings often seem as powerful as they were in ancient history and probably in prehistoric times. Alfred North Whitehead believed that logical philosophy being promoted by the Greeks was derailed by the spread of Christianity, and soon after by Islam. Those who prescribed a faith in religious dogma replaced the brilliant Greek philosophers, Plato and Aristotle, then an abandonment of reason. They created a God in their own image and a Satan to blame for human shortcomings.

These ideas persisted until Gutenberg, with his printing press, introduced reading to the masses, which facilitated the spread of knowledge, unencumbered by religious dogma. As people began to think for themselves, rather than to think only of the ideas handed down by the clergy, technology and the industrial revolution took off.

Although today there are enormous numbers of people who think for themselves, there is still an emotional need to conform to the beliefs of friends, organizations, and those who have celebrity status. The spread of independent thinking has, however, changed society dramatically. Probably mostly for the good.

INNOVATION IN BUSINESS AND LIFE

In Section I we discussed innovation, but it is such an important aspect of science and business that some further stories are warranted.

In science and medicine we look at our innovators with pride. Sometimes they are rewarded with the Nobel Prize.

Section III: Ideas Today

Yet, most of the time innovation is off-limits. Most of us are happy when the ideas people discuss, things we understand, ideas we are familiar with, and concepts from those we admire have been approved by recognized groups. While we claim to believe innovation is very important, it often makes us uncomfortable. We feel better around the institutions and concepts that our group or society has accepted and has lived with for a long time.

Yet, a few commercial innovations will demonstrate how they fit into our culture and our lives, such as POST-IT note pads. Art Fry, a 3M employee, sang in a church choir and the markers he used to locate the pages in his hymnal kept falling out. 3M made scotch tape, which he modified so it would stick just a little, but could easily be removed. After about a dozen years it finally became popular and now is a 200-million-dollar business for 3M.

A book by Tom Peters, *A Passion for Excellence*, provides a model for innovation in business. Usually it takes several levels to make an innovation useful.

Brian Quinn of Dartmouth was lecturing at an AT&T meeting, claiming that nothing new comes from a planning committee. A senior at Bell Labs said this was not true and directed his vice president to give an example. His reply was, *"I've only been in this job thirty years, but I cannot think of a single example where a planning committee came up with a concept that made a difference."*

A Romance with Ideas

Corporations use terms like "breakthrough," "optimization," "systems analysis," and "technology plan" to convince each other they are moving forward. Yet, a realistic look at these efforts reveals they rarely make a difference. Rarely does a Manhattan Project turn out to be as productive as the one that created the atom bomb. This is probably because it is exceedingly rare that an Oppenheimer comes along. Oppenheimer's brilliance and creative ability were manifested as early as his college days, when he decided to learn to read Sanskrit so as to better understand oriental customs and religions.

If we look back at some historical events, it is easy to recognize how wrong organizational reasoning can be. In 1910 the British Secretary of War, after his advisors came to a conclusion, stated, *"We do not consider the aeroplane will be of any use for war purposes."*

In 1930, the French invested billions in the Maginot Line to protect themselves from the Germans. It was flanked in the first few hours when Germany overran France at the beginning of World War II. It was interesting that Charles de Gaulle had predicted this.

The guy who developed Tagamet was but a simple scientist from Glasgow. The pharmaceutical company, Smith Kline, rejected him for several years because of his reputation for being unconventional. A couple of years later he developed a beta-blocker, which was again rejected for four or five years. (Beta-blockers cancel the effect of adrenalin in our circulation.)

Section III: Ideas Today

When Propanolol was finally developed, our recently instituted FDA rejected it for several more years, until it had become popular in England. Prior to its release I had a chance to try it on a teenage girl with hypertrophic cardiomyopathy (an unusual condition resulting in a thickened heart muscle) who was having severe anginal like chest pain. She had instant relief, later went to medical school, and after forty years is still doing well. Beta-blockers have become a billion-dollar-plus product.

These are examples of how difficult it sometimes is to become an innovator. Thank goodness a few stubborn people manage to persist with good ideas. The rapid acceptance of innovative ideas like Google and Facebook tend to suggest that public resistance to new concepts may be less of a problem in the last decade or so, even though our government and many businesses may be lagging behind.

SOME THEORETICAL STUDIES ON INNOVATION

Established concepts compete with disruptive ones. Established concepts help sustainability but are poor at dealing with disruptive ideas.

Disruptive concepts are rarely introduced by senior management. They come from those in the trenches and research efforts. Often these efforts involve many trials that fail. Thus, when senior management recognizes the value of disruptive technologies, the company moves forward. Apple and Steve Jobs are an example of this.

In business, frustrated engineers from established firms often form new companies because management failed to recognize the value of the destructive technologies promoted by their employees. Trial and error is difficult for managers to accept while it can be what keeps those doing the work interested and involved in forward thinking.

It is important to realize that disruptive technology almost always comes from below. That is, from those who are involved in hands-on activities. It is hard for management to understand the utility and progress associated with disruptive technologies.

In business many new companies that develop disruptive technologies result in the failure of established companies when those companies fail to adjust to the needs of customers. So, the customers have a lot to do with the success of companies.

Most of this information has come from an interesting study, *The Innovator's Dilemma*, by Clayton Christensen. However, similar studies have been published by Rebecca Henderson, including *The Reconfiguration of Existing Systems*, and *Failure of Established Firms*. Also published is *The Soul of a New Machine* by Tracy Kidder.

STEVE JOBS: THE IDEA MAN

This remarkable man died of cancer recently at age fifty-seven. The *Economist* calls him a magician. He was the exception to my claims that disruptive ideas come from below.

Section III: Ideas Today

He dropped out of college but had already gotten the computing bug. As a teenager his idol was Bill Hewlett and he talked his way into Hewlett-Packard where he met Steve Wozniak, another computer genius. After spending a few months in India where he became involved in Buddhism and experimented with psychedelic drugs, he returned to the U.S. and co-founded Apple with Steve Wozniak. The Mac computer, which they created, became very popular, but after he was fired it almost failed. Only after 1996 when he was hired back did they begin to prosper and soon they created the iMac, the iPod, the iPhone, and the iPad. By 2005 Apple was financially the most successful company in the United States. Jobs said, *"Technology is not enough. It has to be married with liberal arts and with the humanities that produce results that make our hearts sing."*

Now that he is gone it remains to be seen if the ideas of his successors can match his magic. It has been said that innovation is the lifeblood of our economy and is the strategic priority of CEOs everywhere. There is little doubt that the U.S. has had, and still has, more innovators than any other country. Jeff Dyer, the author of *The Innovator's DNA*, has identified the five skills of disruptive innovators: questioning, observing, networking, experimenting, and associational thinking. Those who would like to study these ideas in detail should read his recent book published by Harvard Business Review Press.

THE EMERGENCE OF GRANDPARENTS

Most of us know how our grandparents influenced our life and culture. They helped us orient to our surroundings and society. They helped us appreciate our environment, our family, and the institutions that influenced our way of life. Many of us recognize their importance and look to grandparents as important members of our society. But this was not always so.

Until about 30,000 years ago, humans rarely lived long enough to become grandparents. An interesting study by Rachel Caspari in *Scientific American* reviews her studies of over twenty years that explain how humans began to survive more than twenty years only 30,000 years ago. She examined teeth from the fossil record that revealed survival began to increase near the end of the Neanderthal's replacement by modern Homo sapiens. These studies revealed how important the contributions of older members of society to culture and progress became. About 10,000 years ago their numbers exploded and with this increase the innovations that led to the complex culture of today. It may be difficult for many in today's youth-oriented culture to accept the importance of grandparents, but anyone who loves to study scholarly material will soon recognize the importance of this group in our society.

THE INFLUENCE OF SOCIAL HIERARCHY

Most of us are aware that dominant hierarchies occur in social species, especially in primates. How does rank influence physiology and health? In most primates the social organization is based on dominance. In stable situations the most dominant individual has been shown to have the least stress, but when a challenge to boundaries occurs, the most dominant temporarily experiences the most stress. This seems to be the case in human social situations where coronary artery disease is very common in those of lower social status but is less common in captains of industry and situations where power is handed down through inheritance.

In human society the stress of a menial job can often be overcome by dominance in an organization, such as a deacon in a church or by being emotionally titillated by being a fan of a professional sports figure or organization, or of a celebrity entertainer. A recent lecture by Lee Lipsenthal, a member of the Ornish group, presented interesting data on how social support protects against CAD (coronary artery disease) and how important it is to engage in pleasurable social situations to insure a healthy, happy life. Physicians would all be better if they did all in their power to be aware of the social aspects of their patients and to convince them that they are their friends. The same could be said for teachers and managers and most people of authority. Most preachers know this instinctively.

PROGRESS OF HUMANITY, MAYBE

Stephen J. Gould, a brilliant scientist, had some interesting ideas. He claims progress does not pervade or mark the history of life. The origin of Homo sapiens should be viewed as an accidental rather than an expected consequence. We should give up the conventional notion of human dominance as preordained. We must all conform to what we call the laws of nature.

In 1868 Thomas Huxley claimed, "*The chessboard is the world, the pieces are phenomena of the universe and the rules of the game are what we call the laws of nature.*"

Science is but common sense. We must realize that nature always wins. How did we rise to our present civilized state at what we believe is the peak of the tree of life? Were we meant to be here, or are we just lucky?

We now believe with considerable certainty that we probably evolved from trilobites in the Cambrian Sea, from simple multi-celled organisms, to dinosaurs in the Mesozoic Age, to our present form with the largest cerebral cortex of any animal. In the face of this evolution, invertebrates did not die out. We just wedged in. Today, more than half of all vertebrates (more than 20,000 living species) are still fish.

People continually portray our little stream of vertebrate life as the model of evolution. A realistic concept is that our one stream is part of the torrent of life, a concept that has been reinforced every year since Darwin published the *Origin of the Species* in 1859. For hundreds of years we believed life continued to progress and humans, at its apex, were continuing that trend.

Gould has proposed an interesting argument that significant progress has reached or maybe is near to this apex. Gould's beliefs on this issue were printed in *Evolution of Smarts*.

He claims that if progress is so good, why don't we see more of it? Not a very scientific statement, but it is easy to wonder about progress when we see what seems to be the deterioration of social progress, the conflict and murder throughout the world. There is a lack of appreciation for things many of us consider beautiful.

There is little doubt civilization and society are becoming more complex, what with the Internet, cell phones, and our mechanical devices. You can judge whether it is getting better. I believe our standard of living exceeds any time in history.

INTERPERSONAL BEHAVIOR

How we interact with those around us, with our family, our social friends, and our colleagues at work is one of the most important aspects of our lives. It has long been recognized that we often find what we expect to find in people and thus expectancies play an enormous role in our personal relationships. In 1968, Rosenthal and Jacobs reported on an experiment where teachers were led to believe that a certain number of their sixth grade students would blossom academically. Unbeknownst to the teachers, the students had been randomly chosen. After a year it was determined that those randomly chosen actually tested better than those not chosen.

This leads to the concept of a self-fulfilling prophecy, which has been validated over and over. Of course, our expectations are influenced by prior experiences. We classify people as stereotypes because of a first impression, which limits our ability to understand those in our environment.

I believe the "take home message" from this material is that we must try to expect the best from those with whom we interact. On the other hand, we should be realistic and appreciate what others stand for and are capable of doing. We should not expect more than is possible. If we practice this routinely, we will be popular with our peers and more successful in interpersonal relationships.

SOME IDEAS ABOUT OUR CULTURE

A robust attachment to individual freedom and rational skeptical inquiry has driven technological, scientific, and commercial innovation since the Dark Ages. Prior civilization has usually been driven by loyalties associated with religion and race. When you are born into a way of life, the values of that culture usually determine how you feel about issues, what you eat, how you dress, and what you believe.

Mahatma Gandhi suggested that although Plato, Jesus, Galileo, Mozart, and Einstein (all products of the West) were not frauds or fools, their beliefs and teachings had not guided the thoughts and behaviors of enough people. We all know his history.

Section III: Ideas Today

The rich accomplishments of China, Islam, or the West are not really in conflict. The problem that ignorance and barbarism often masquerade as loyalty to a civilization or religion is too common. Prejudice is really the inability to recognize the merits of another person or ideology. It is too common that social and religious groups will demonize those who disagree. We now have less cultural authority, which mandates that we tolerate and even admire aberrant behavior. Just the opposite from the Middle Ages, when the Catholic Church persecuted and often tortured those who failed to conform to the dogma of the time. This tolerance is almost certainly good, as time will tell.

It is interesting how beliefs change. The Greek philosophers, such as Socrates, sat about the marketplace questioning, arguing, and patiently exploring ideas. Their ideas suggested that you should practice self-examination and free inquiry, and we should strive to get rid of ignorance, to see things as others see them. Although this is an ideal that we accept, it must be mixed with practical matters, such as making a living and building some sort of estate or security. The ideas of Socrates are all too uncommon today, however.

When we read the daily newspaper, the real world overwhelms us at times. Climate change, mortgage stress, political corruption, crime, greed, ignorance, pollution, and terrorism all seem to dominate our culture. This should not divert our efforts from trying to create a little segment where the beauty of relationships, love, truth, and our quality of life can flourish.

Was security found by those who were hippies pursuing creative freedom? We can all remember the so-called free way of life sought by those who dropped out of society in the 1960s, mainly in response to their objection to authority and the Vietnam War. Where are they today? Did they find happiness by rejecting the society of their parents and peers? It would appear that their experiment failed the test of time. Their progeny might be those who are presently occupying Wall Street and other financial centers.

Section IV

The Future of Ideas

A GLOBAL GOVERNMENT

This is an idea that has been debated by many of the best minds in the world, so I don't intend to give definite answers but, because it is so important, I decided to discuss it in the hope that my readers will give it some thought as it may affect us and our children in a profound way.

The history of this idea goes back centuries to the invasions of Western society by Genghis Khan and by Attila the Hun, who almost overran Rome, and slightly later by the Qin Emperor of China, who dominated Asia. Later it reflects the Hapsburg family in Europe, the Spanish in the New World, and for a while even the British with their far-flung colonies. These early attempts were all top-down systems where the power was concentrated in a single man or government. For a

A Romance with Ideas

short while it even looked like Hitler's Germany might achieve dominance, at least over Europe.

After World War I, at the Treaty of Versailles, Woodrow Wilson proposed the League of Nations in 1919, possibly the first attempt to design an international government that was based on the voluntary decisions of those governed. The failure of the U.S. to become part of this dashed any chance for success. A quarter of a century later, after the Second World War, a conference led by President Truman in San Francisco founded the United Nations. This has turned out to be the most long-lasting attempt but has many weaknesses and has marginal support in some sectors.

Some of its weaknesses include the design. The controlling body, the Security Council, has two countries that often derail the best of plans. These countries are Russia and China, which commonly veto the proposals of the remaining members. Also, because the United Nations has no military force of their own, when they vote to intervene in conflicts that to Americans and most Europeans are serious, the U.N. must rely on various countries to contribute troops and aircraft. Many times these members cannot be counted on. It has also been unable to curtail the spread of nuclear weapons, a technology introduced by the U.S. in 1945, as a way to convince Japan that to continue the war against the U.S. was untenable. It worked. Japan surrendered in short order. However, such a device could not be contained. At present there are nine or

Section IV: The Future of Ideas

ten countries with nuclear weapons: the United States, China, the United Kingdom, Russia, France, India, Pakistan, North Korea, and Israel, with Iran probably soon. This will spread over the next few years, and the peaceful intentions of some of these countries, including Iran and North Korea, are in serious doubt. There is little chance any of the troublemakers will give up their weapons in the foreseeable future.

So, what are the chances of a global government? The most recent attempt at combining many countries has been the European Union, which is nearing bankruptcy.

To date the United Nations has been unable to prevent genocide. In 1995, 800,000 Rwandans were slaughtered in about six months. Several countries have also developed a hydrogen bomb 750 times more powerful than the one used at Hiroshima. The United Nations is often dysfunctional; the Kremlin used its veto power 119 times between 1945 and 1991 and since then has continued to use it regularly. In spite of 63,000 employees in the U.N., almost all are loyal to their home base, and it has been said many are spies, using the U.N. as an entry to the United States. Although the stated goals of the U.N. are laudable, they are far from being able to solve many of the world problems. These include poverty, terrorism, genocide, and major wars. There may be a time when global government will be a realistic solution to the above problems, but in the near future fear of retribution seems to be the most effective strategy. Maybe when my grandchildren have grandchildren, a more effective United Nations will be able to deal with most of the issues we have discussed. At this time there seems to be little advantage served by our membership.

Human nature, which tends to pit us against them, is far from overcome. Although we have made progress in the last 100 years, unfortunately I believe global government is a long way off.

An excellent reference on this subject is Strobe Talbott's book *The Great Experiment*.

THE DEATH OF COMMON SENSE

This stimulating book by attorney Philip K. Howard was first published in 1994 and subsequently republished and lauded by dozens of publications, including the *New York Times Book Review*, the *Wall Street Journal*, and newspapers from cities all over America. Howard goes into great detail to describe how our laws, often hundreds of pages long, have paralyzed government and private industry and destroyed individual freedom and the government's and private people's right to make sensible decisions. He points out that it is now impossible to fire an incompetent employee in government and government-funded agencies, such as our school system. Old laws that have outlasted their usefulness are almost never repealed. The cost and delay of decisions, due to our smothering legal system, paralyzes government and private enterprise alike.

Section IV: The Future of Ideas

The legal goal of making everything fair and eliminating diversity is stifling progress. America is drowning in lawsuits and endless red tape. Protecting ourselves from the law and lawsuits is costing hundreds of millions of dollars every day. Does no one want to remedy this mess?

The U.S. Supreme Court, in about 2006, reversed the 100-year-old tradition that foreign nationals who attacked the U.S. were not entitled to American courts when they were held outside the United States; i.e., in Guantanamo Bay. For the first time the court ruled against our Secretary of Defense, Donald Rumsfeld. It was the first time in history that the Secretary of Defense lost a case in the Supreme Court against an admitted terrorist.

Fortunately, a few months later Congress passed the Military Commissions Act, defining an unlawful enemy combatant, reauthorizing the military's right to hold terrorists and try them in a military court. Up to now this has not been overturned. In spite of this, every aspect of U.S. military operations have to contend with legal traps set by our enemies, as well as by our own citizens. This new threat has been termed "lawfare." Donald Rumsfeld, Secretary of Defense, claimed this binds the "American Gulliver," making us less able to defend our citizens and our military against those who hate America. Henry Kissinger reported in 2001 that he was still facing legal action for incidents that occurred when he had been working for the Nixon administration thirty years prior.

Belgium, in 1990, passed a law that it could bring legal action considered to be "crimes against humanity" anywhere in the world. Fortunately, because of the threat to move NATO headquarters out of Belgium, they repealed the law.

Lawfare has been inhibited, some by common sense, but is still a threat to us all.

ECONOMICS—THE BOURGEOIS VIRTUE

A book review by Deirdre McCloskey takes issue with those who are hostile to capitalism. She points out that many of our academics and so-called intellectuals share this belief. They label the middle class as "bourgeois," a term implying mediocrity. She also points out that as capitalism has expanded, slavery has been eliminated, women have been emancipated, and universities have been built. Under capitalism, society is not divided into friends and enemies since the free market requires respect for both the provider and recipient of goods.

Under capitalism even those in the lowest income group live better than the royalty of the seventeenth century. The products of entrepreneurs, many of whom are supported by capitalism, benefit us all. *Forbes* recently reported that one company, Apple, propelled by the leadership of Steve Jobs, added $360 billion to our society over a thirty-year period. One innovative company, under the leadership of one innovative man. What a contribution! Think of how many people in the world have cell phones. Almost all those who camped out

Section IV: The Future of Ideas

in Wall Street and other economic centers recently had cell phones but hated the companies that made them possible.

Not only do corporations make it possible for all of the myriads of inventions that have improved the life of everyone to be manufactured at a cost that most people can afford, but they have paid millions in taxes that supports our spendthrift government. Also, those who have reaped enormous profits have often contributed immeasurably to the quality of life. One of the most remarkable has been Bill Gates, retired chief of Microsoft. His money and influence have resulted in a reduction in death and suffering all over the world by stimulating the pharmaceutical companies to produce vaccines. These have already reduced the incidence of pneumonia, rotavirus (a leading cause of diarrhea and death worldwide), and meningitis and may soon result in a vaccine for malaria, which is responsible for at least one million deaths a year.

Although Bill Gates has done the most to benefit society with the money earned by a corporation, captains of industry have been involved in this type of activity for generations. Those who do not recognize this, such as the present occupiers who demonstrate against corporate America, are by their recent actions advertising their colossal stupidity and ignorance.

Over the years, anyone who is interested in ideas sooner or later will try to learn something about economics. Of course, economics and the economy are so intertwined with politics today that political theory and economics seem inseparable.

For hundreds of years economic decisions were made by warlords and kings who were only marginally interested in the welfare of the common man. Within those kingdoms there evolved a few city-states where people could earn a living by developing a skill that was uncommon and useful. As these centers of industry evolved and became more influential, what is now recognized as free enterprise became more common and probably led to what we now call a democracy. The independence of the United States from the kingdoms of Europe gave birth to our representative government, and to the freedom that allowed our economic system to outpace the older forms of government in the rest of the world. Over the years the obvious inefficiencies of this type of organization became over-emphasized, which created the concept that experts in government would be more efficient and that we should delegate most governmental functions to those experts. This led to the beliefs in socialism and communism. In the 1930s and 40s, as the U.S. and western Europe rebelled against these concepts, von Hayek from Austria and Ayn Rand became the modern advocates of the so-called free market economy, and from the eighteenth century on this process had been proliferating rapidly.

Today, many believe too much power is granted to corporations and that the government should protect us from their influence.

Is there a better system that treats the majority of our citizens fairly? Is there a perfect form of government?

Section IV: The Future of Ideas

In America we now have a chance to critically analyze how a very powerful government system has functioned, not only in the U.S. but in western Europe as well. In a societal effort to better provide for those who are relatively unproductive, a financial meltdown is developing. Can the rich countries and people generate enough wealth to correct the problem?

Any analysis of how to deal with problems leads to the conclusion that they make mistakes. Lots of mistakes. But when these mistakes become obvious, most people learn from them.

Anyone who studies innovation, which has done more to increase the well-being of our people, realizes that most of our progress comes from recognizing mistakes and then moving on to come up with a new approach. Our free enterprise system and our capitalism continue to make mistakes, but we soon learn they are mistakes and abandon the bad ideas. Hayek states, "It's always from a minority acting in a way different from what a majority would prescribe that the majority learns to do better."

The most important form of learning does not always take place in discussions with others, or to arrive at a consensus, as popular as that is. It comes from recognizing our own failures or the failures of those around us, and correcting them.

Mark Pennington, a professor of politics at the University of London, claims, "An economy is robust if it is able to withstand various stresses and strains."

Human rationality and human imperfections, especially limited benevolence, are so common that our system needs to overcome these shortcomings. So far, central planning, which establishes rules and laws that restrict our behavior and ability to alter our course of action, has failed to deal with many of the realities of our financial world.

It is hoped that as more people understand the basic concepts discussed here, our economic and political systems will evolve to a point that we all can recognize as becoming mutually beneficial.

THE RUSH TO THE CITIES

A recent issue of *Scientific American* featured a story claiming that the world's population is migrating toward cities. There is little doubt that this trend is everywhere, and according to the authors, it is for the better. Because I grew up in a small town and have spent most of my life in a small city, I am saddened by this trend. On the other hand, there seems little doubt that there are many reasons why this is so.

People enjoy being with others. People in cities earn more money than in small towns or rural areas. Research seems conclusive that intense frequent social interactions correlate with higher productivity and more innovations, as well as economic pressure that weeds out inefficiencies. These trends attract more talent so that the increasing population drives up rents and property values. Some cities

Section IV: The Future of Ideas

have a reputation for cutting-edge novelty and a culture of excellence that attracts more people, which drives financial progress. Certain cities develop a reputation for these traits that persists for years. For example, San Francisco and Boston are richer than their size would suggest, whereas Phoenix, Arizona, and Riverside, California, continue to be poorer and attract fewer people and resources. Also, there is a recent trend suggesting the denser cities tend to be "greener" and have more efficient public transportation and other types of urban infrastructure.

At present in America, the optimum population seems to be somewhere around ten million. However, the enormous cities of India and China fail to fit this mold, probably because of the poverty and lack of education. In Latin America 70% of the people live in cities. In the developed countries and Bangalore, Dharai, Mumbai in India, and Rio de Janeiro, Brazil, the migration to the cities continues. In the nineteenth century, London was the only city with a population of five million. Now there are fifty-four cities, most of them in Asia.

It has been claimed that even though enormous slums still characterize many cities, many claim that cities are the best way to reduce poverty without wrecking the planet. In his book *Green Metropolis*, David Owen reports that in cities, roads, sewers, and power lines are shorter and therefore use fewer resources. Their apartments take less energy to heat and cool and light than do houses. People in dense cities drive less. In crowded cities like New York, the per capita energy use and carbon emissions are below the national average.

One example of successful urbanization is Seoul, the capital of South Korea. Between 1960 and 2000 the population increased from three million to ten million. At the same time, South Korea went from being a very poor country, with per capita GDP of $100, to one of the richest countries.

Only time will tell whether this trend to larger cities will continue, but at present there seems little doubt that cities all over the world are on this trajectory.

EDUCATION AND THE SIGNIFICANCE OF LIFE

Every now and then we come across an article or a book that presents ideas that are somewhat unique. Such a book by Jiddu Krishnamurti was published in 1953 in England and republished in New York in 1981. Some of his ideas are worth presenting although, as I point out, may be idealistic and impractical.

He starts by pointing out that most parents and teachers do not like to foster discontent because it disrupts all forms of security. Parents and teachers encourage the acceptance of our culture and beliefs when young people are often most likely to have a desire to inquire, to ask tough questions, and to encourage unconventional ideas. Unfortunately, most adults try to shape their children so that they will gratify their desires,

Section IV: The Future of Ideas

vanities, and idiosyncrasies. If we all encouraged our children to be compassionate and be accepting of different belief systems, religions, cultures, and lifestyles, it would lead to a reduction in strife and a more peaceful world. He believes few of us understand ourselves. In our effort to conform to our culture, we are often frustrated and seek escape through politics, sex, alcohol, or various religions. He believes conformity is often due to a desire for security and stimulated by fear of being unconventional. Thus, we accept authority and fail to ask questions that might reveal new insights, new self-knowledge, and reduce conflict.

There is a natural craving for certainty, for security, that inhibits self-knowledge and prevents an open mind. Krishnamurti claims our system of education, which produces scientists, engineers, executives, and other specialists, generates competition and separatism. This reduces tolerance of those who fail to achieve standards we set for our neighbors or ourselves. We also vest authority in politicians and others who are anointed by our media as being celebrities. This generates a policy of ranking people, not because they are compassionate or truthful or tolerant but because they fit someone's standards that are arbitrarily determined by our "leaders." These leaders are often people with traits that break down tolerance and understanding of our fellow citizens. The leaders promote the concept that a particular class or religion or race or political party is superior, which generates conflict. As we all are aware, this often leads to violence or warfare.

My comments: His ideas are worth considering; however, no culture, religion, or government has succeeded in incorporating most of them into our lives. Why? Because our culture and behavior have evolved over thousands of years, and because it has conformed to our inherited ways of dealing with our fellow man and our environment. I am sure all of us realize our present culture is far from perfect. Will we evolve toward a more tolerant, loving, happy way of dealing with each other? Maybe, but we certainly have a long way to go.

UNDERSTANDING ISLAM

At the present time, in 2012, understanding anything as political and as loaded with emotion as the Muslim religion is not easy for those not raised in an Arab country. In the United States, which is so predominantly Christian, the most popular way to be misinformed is to read the newspapers.

A recent report lists America's Muslim population at 2,595,000, which is 0.8% of our citizens. The attack on the World Trade Centers has polarized our public opinion and probably that of many countries so that facts are somewhat difficult to come by. For those who would like to study this issue in depth, R. Stephen Humphreys has an impressive list of studies and publications. Humphreys is a professor of Islamic studies at the University of California, Santa Barbara.

When one sums up the combined reports there is little doubt that Americans have concluded the radical or terrorist

Section IV: The Future of Ideas

element is a powerful force and either supported or tolerated by many Muslims. However, authorities claim that these beliefs are overblown. The majority of the 2.5 million Muslims of our population are almost universally against violence and by any standards are good citizens. In spite of their support for terrorism, almost all seem to support the concept that they seek to establish a system where a theocratic government imposes and enforces Sharia (Muslim holy law). It would appear that Muslims reject democracy, civil liberties, and laws made by men. However, the "Arab Spring," the uprising in Egypt, Libya, and other Muslim countries, is evidence that there is an upsurge in desire for more education, better economic opportunities, and a less rigid social system than that proscribed by radical Islam.

It seems likely that the younger people in the Arab world, who comprise at least 40% of the world's population, would like to live peacefully with the rest of us. There is evidence that they still believe that they practice the true religion but a variety that can co-exist with the non-Muslim world.

RECONSIDERING BENEVOLENCE

The book *What's Wrong with Benevolence* by David Stove, an insightful Australian philosopher, introduced an idea that is intriguing but somewhat depressing. His conclusions are difficult to argue with and I am inclined to wish that which he claims is not so.

Benevolence, he claims, was not a natural belief or culturally popular until some time after Christianity became widespread. Even then, although it was recommended by the church, it was not universally practiced.

Utopian schemes to reorganize society and eliminate poverty are relatively recent and have regularly ended in failure. The most important example is twentieth-century communism. The emotional fuel of the revolutionaries has almost always been a passionate desire to alleviate or abolish misery. As we all know, it has been such a monumental failure that millions suffered and died under its influence. Yet Karl Marx and Joseph Stalin were never convinced. They believed, or preached, that any privilege and advantage of one person over another was morally wrong, especially that of owning property. "The fruits of the earth belong to all" was the claim.

Yet, some very wise men, as early as 1788, including Joseph Priestly, claimed, "If every man who is reduced to poverty be allowed to have a claim on the common stock of substance, he will be improvident, spending everything he gets in the most extravagant manner. The greater provision we make for the poor, the more poor there will be. Thus, man, instead of being the most provident of animals, as he naturally would be, becomes the most improvident of them all."

In England, after the poor laws were instituted, the tax burden consistently increased and the number of those who were recipients of the money also consistently increased. This has been the experience all over the Western world. Thus, the attempts to redistribute wealth results in the opposite of happiness it is intended to produce.

A solution for this problem would be to remove benevolence from the government but encourage it as a private way to demonstrate our concern for our fellow man. Thus, it would insulate those who are productive from the enormous burdens of a benevolent government.

Although Stove's arguments make sense, they have little chance of being accepted in the foreseeable future.

Appendix and Essays

APPENDIX #1

Concepts worth remembering from colleagues and authors:

- "Science progresses by hunch, vision and intuition. Culture influences what we see and how we see it." — Gould

- "Men who have excessive faith in their theories or ideas are ill-prepared to make discoveries and are poor observers." — Claud Bernard

- "Credible discoveries are those we can assimilate, validate, corroborate and verify." —

- William James

- "Columbus thought he knew where he was going, where he arrived, and where he had been. All wrong, yet it led to an important discovery."

- "Some of the most powerful experiences man can have are his interest in the mysterious and the elation of final understanding."

- "Progress comes when intuition and passion meet objectively with logic." — Grinnel

- "Discovery is impossible. What man does not know, he does not know what to look for." — Plato, 2000 years ago. No one ever told Plato about serendipity.

- "We live in a society exquisitely dependent on science and technology in which hardly anyone knows anything about science and technology." — Carl Sagan

- "Most of the information I have was acquired looking for something else." — Art Riedel, Portland businessman

- "Minds are like parachutes. They only function when open."

- "Ideals are like stars; you can't touch them, but like a sailor at sea, you use them as guides. Following them will help you reach your destiny."

- "Worry is like a rocking chair. It will give you something to do but it won't get you anywhere."

- "The wise man doesn't expect to find life worth living; he makes it that way."

Appendix and Essays

- "We have no more right to consume happiness without producing it than to consume wealth without producing it." **Comment**: Try to tell this to those who occupy Wall Street.

- "A government that robs Peter to pay Paul can always count on the support of Paul."

APPENDIX #2

Sidney Harris, after reviewing *A History of the World*, a 100-page book by the historian Roberts, had this to say, "There are no comprehensive solutions to the world's economic, political, religious or cultural problems. Most people don't know exactly what they are for but might have a better idea about what they are against. Life is full of unresolved contradictions. Contrariness in people is almost the only invariable we can count on. About all we should strive for is to find a series of compromises."

APPENDIX #3

Ideas from William C. Roberts' book *Facts and Ideas from Anywhere*:

- "The measure of man is not where he stands in moments of comfort and convenience, but where he stands at times of controversy and challenge." — Martin Luther King

A Romance with Ideas

- "The telephone book is full of facts but it doesn't contain a single idea." — Mortiner Adler

- "The secret that has led me to my goal, my strength lies solely in my tenacity." — Louis Pasteur

- "Every great advance in knowledge has involved the rejection of authority." — Thomas Huxley

- "An institution can be the length and shadow of one man." — Ralph Waldo Emerson

- "Genius is 1% inspiration and 99% perspiration." — Thomas Edison

- "Great genius disdains the beaten path. It sees a region hitherto unexplored." — Abraham Lincoln

- "The greater the ignorance, the greater the dogmatism." — William Osler

THE NEED TO SUFFER
(Written in 1973)

Not long ago I happened to overhear a conversation between two boys relating the terrible persecution they had to endure because of their long hair. The ring of sublime satisfaction in the vivid description of their suffering irritated me. When I related this to my wife, I concluded that this was another proof of their distorted view of life. It was only a few hours later, however, that I found myself relating to friends,

Appendix and Essays

with great relish, how uncomfortable I had been on a camping trip on the Colorado River. How could I, a well-adjusted adult, be acting just like those funky kids? I wondered if unhappiness and pain were necessary for all of us. Why do we, when ostensibly laboring for generations to eliminate pain from our society, seem always to fail?

It might be in order to look at some of the personality traits and see how they fit into or mold our present society. What human personality traits or emotional needs play a dominant role in today's social order? How have these personality traits led into our present social organizational structures?

1. The need to be somebody, the need to have tomorrow. Ernie Pyle relates that as he sat in a briefing room during World War II where pilots were planning to go on a mission in which few expected to return, the thing that he noticed among these men was not their fear of death but their reluctance to give up life, the reluctance to give up the future. This must be the most powerful instinct in humans as well as more primitive animals.

2. The need to know is an emotion more common the higher one goes in the phylogenetic tree. Curiosity, of course, has been noted in many primitive animals and is extremely important in the great apes but is certainly at its highest form in the human. Need for self-analysis, however, is not found in animals as far as we can tell, even though it is a powerful drive in humans.

A Romance with Ideas

3. The need to experience joy or happiness. One might jump to the conclusion that this is the most important of all of our present needs from the appearance of the way we live. Many philosophers have stated that this is really the only important human aim, and of course many things contribute to this, such as material things, interpersonal relationships, belief in ourselves, sex, food, and so on. Certainly the need for a close one-to-one relationship with some other individual or individuals is very important.

4. The trait which is overlooked by most philosophers and most social planners and which is apparently out of style in our present-day society is the need to suffer. It is of interest that it is not developed to any degree. We shall examine this concept as we go along, but first let us discuss some of the important religious movements that dominate the earth at this time, because they have had such a far-reaching effect on our social institutions. Most of the major religions, which seem to influence man and be part of his present-day culture, were all established as institutions about the same time, in a broad sense.

Hinduism: This is the oldest of the major religions, having been established about 2500 B.C., and still has an enormous influence in Asia. There are probably about five million people practicing some form of Hinduism; although we are not very

Appendix and Essays

aware of its impact on our Western civilization, it is gaining in popularity with our youth.

Dr. Oppenheimer, who grew up under the Judeo-Christian influence and was the one person who probably had the most to do with the detonation of the atomic bomb, relates this story. As he was waiting for the countdown of the first bomb, he recalled these lines: "I am death, the shatterer of worlds. Waiting that hour it ripens to their doom." These lines are not from the Bible or the Koran or Shakespeare but from the Bhagaved Gita, the most important of the holy books of the Hindu religion. Most of us in America don't become involved much in the Hindu faith. What does it represent?

There are three main gods: Brahman, lord of creation; Vishnu, lord of preservation; and Shiva, god of destruction and recreation. They exhort their followers to reject materialism, physical power, and physical gratification and to develop the ability to bear pain. The Hindu pursues Nirvana or Artman, the inner power that links him with the universe, denying him worldly pleasures. Formulators of this ancient religion, which was well established at the time Moses was climbing Mt. Sinai to receive the Ten Commandments, recognized the human need for suffering. An enormous pantheon of minor Hindu deities and prophets evolved to emphasize this concept among the loyal followers. Attempts to materially intervene in natural things were discouraged. A very passive philosophy resulted.

Buddhism: About 500 B.C. Buddha, who grew up as a Hindu and was the son of a very wealthy prince, became disturbed by what he considered to be perversion of the original teachings of the Hindu faith. In much the same way as Martin Luther, he disagreed with the established church and eventually started a new religious sect. Buddha, which is translated to "I am awake" in Sanskrit, taught basically the same concept of self-sacrifice and suffering and attempted to return his followers to the simple ideas of the original Hindu teachings. He rejected his worldly riches and practiced a Spartan religious life, emphasizing the importance of self-reliance, and above all the rejection of the desires of the ego, such as price, avarice, and greed.

"By ourselves is evil done. By ourselves we pain endure. By ourselves we cease from wrong. By ourselves become we pure. No one saves us but ourselves. No one can and no one may. We ourselves must tread the path. Buddha only shows the way."

This ascetic way of life, which eulogizes self-denial, developed an enormous following. Buddha rejected most of the trappings of organized Hinduism and even rejected the presence of a hereafter or a symbolic god in the sense of the Hindus, Christian, or Jewish beliefs. Buddhism spread to Japan in force but had a very moderate influence on China. It dominated southeast Asia where it still holds sway. Buddha must have recognized the human need for rejection of pleasure and some inner need for some type of suffering.

Confucianism: About the same time that Buddha was preaching his religion, another great teacher was spreading quaint sayings across China. He denied our classic idea of a deity or a life hereafter. Confucius was of humble birth but had an uncanny ability to influence people with his homey sayings, emphasizing the importance of establishing interpersonal relationships and subjugating himself to the needs and desires of others. His concept of personal sacrifice to those around him profoundly influenced the customs of China for twenty-five centuries. His simple stories have been a source of Western humor for years. However, for 2,000 years until the time of the Communist takeover of China, every Chinese child learned verses from Confucius rather than stories about Dick and Jane as we do in the United States.

At the time of Mao Tse-tung's takeover of China, there were about 500 million (1/5 of the world's population) still practicing the customs taught by this humble teacher. Basically, it is very similar to Hinduism and Buddhism in that personal sacrifice played a very important role. It is of special interest that communism that replaced it preaches personal sacrifice for the good of the state.

Judaism: Turning to the western part of Asia we find the mother religion of the West, Judaism. It very likely evolved from the moral concepts first recorded in the fifth Egyptian dynasty, and records of their beliefs date back to about 2600 B.C. A text promoting monotheism attributed to Ptahotep, who was the advisor to Ming Issy, was only deciphered a few years ago. Also, about 1500 B.C., somewhere near the time the Jews are said to have made their Exodus, Amenhotep IV, the child king who married his fabled sister Nefertiti, started the West's first monotheistic religion. At his direction, the sun god replaced all the other deities in the Nile Valley and for a short period demanded the Egyptians turn away from pomp and splendor and follow the simple life. With the death of Amenhotep the displaced priests of Ra soon ended the child king's dream.

The Spartan faith of the wandering Jewish tribes set the stage for the profound influences of Christianity and Islam. The basic difference between these religions and those of the East may be established by the line from Genesis, "Let them (God says of the men he will create) have dominion over all the Earth," while Confucius says, "Those who would take over the earth and shape it to their will, never, I notice, succeed."

In spite of the Judeo-Christian emphasis on human dominance over nature, the early Israelites certainly believed in sacrifice. Under the command of Yahweh, Abraham went to the land of Moriah to offer his only son Isaac as a burnt offering. David, the King of the Jews, sought to pacify God by the sacrifice of seven of the sons of Saul during a siege. The Christian God, of course, sacrificed his son Jesus to save our souls, and the emphasis by the Christians of the original sin, therefore insisting on sacrifice to lift this burden from our people, plays a major role.

The preoccupation of the early Christians with martyrs somewhat reminds us of our present interest in the martyred

Appendix and Essays

political heroes of modern America. Predating the sacrifices of the Judeo-Christian and Muslim movements were the sacrifices of animals in Egypt, which were of course valuable property. Unlike the worshippers of Moloch in Mesopotamia and the Sinai Peninsula, human sacrifice was rarely invoked. Circumcision, which is symbolic of sacrifice and bloodletting, was practiced as far back as 4000 B.C. in Egypt and probably was spread from Egypt by the Jews in their great exodus. When the King of Moab was besieged by the Israelites, he burned his first son to gain support from the gods. What greater sacrifice is there?

The early Greeks and Romans both demanded sacrifices. The cruelty of the Romans, who vicariously suffered as they watched men and women killed by wild animals, is well known. Paul, the founder of modern Christianity, grew up in the Greek village of Tarsus. It was in this village that a festival was annually practiced, celebrating the virgin birth of a young man designated as a god who was finally sacrificed so that he might gain immortality. Each year in Tarsus a young man was selected to symbolically represent this god and was sacrificed amid great celebration.

If we transport ourselves to the advancing cultures in Central and South America we find the Mayans of Guatemala and the Aztecs of Mexico actively engaged in human sacrifices as late as the time of the Spanish conquistadors. Why is it that all early human cultures systematically included suffering and sacrifice? Wasn't life hard enough without that?

What of modern man? What evidence do we find that humans need to suffer in our own society? There hardly seems a time when we have not been engaged in war. If not to conquer some other country, theoretically to protect someone from aggression. Wars lead not only to personal sacrifice but also to national sacrifice. In our modern sports not only do people revel in the suffering of the athletes as they did in Rome, but emotionally they attach themselves to the career of professional teams just to share the suffering of their defeat, as well as the exhilaration of their victories. Our high school and college fraternities require suffering during an initiation. The young people seem to enjoy it. Why is it that many affluent sons of our present society reject their culture on behalf of a radical movement? Are things too good? Do they need the pain of an uncertain cause?

In the 60s I wandered into a hippy encampment along the Colorado River and sat down and listened for hours to their conversations. They unswervingly kept to a single subject, describing to each other the various ways that the establishment had persecuted them. While relating this persecution the look of ecstasy on their faces was amazing. What a wonderful experience describing this terrible treatment that had been perpetrated upon them. Think of us. How often have we reveled in the recitation of a period of emotional or physical pain? "Let me tell you about my operation."

Why, at this time of unprecedented material plenty and affluence, does our society seem to be bursting apart? Why are our children rejecting our values and our institutions? No such process is taking place in the primitive or underdeveloped countries. They still have enough obligated suffering.

It may be that when Homo sapiens evolved to their present form, their chromosomes carried some emotional needs that we have overlooked. Needs that were instinctively recognized by the ancients. It may be that we cannot stand too much happiness, too much security. Hedonism, the search for happiness, may be a false god. It would appear that by trying to take away pain and suffering from our children and our friends, we have robbed ourselves, and our families, of a need as important as love, as important as sex. So, what has happened? Our children are seeking unhappiness, our newspaper reporters and other media are engulfing us with news of unhappiness, and we are involving ourselves in sports and organizations that can make us unhappy. It would almost appear, if one looks at it realistically, that we are a race of masochists. We are running away from, and after pain, simultaneously. Sacrifice, pain, and suffering come naturally to primitive societies and could not be avoided. Therefore, we genetically evolved, not only to be able to live it, but to depend on it.

Unless we recognize the importance of pain and strife, unless we deliberately allot it a place in our lives, in our culture, our social order, we may destroy ourselves in search for pain. The evolution of man has been too slow to adapt to a painless world. Let us wake up to this fact while there is still time.

When asked to preach a sermon in the Cal Heights Methodist Church by the minister Paul Woudenberg in 1973, I used this theme as my text. It was not very well received.

THE GREEKS STARTED ALL THE TROUBLE... THE CULT OF INDIVIDUALISM

When the American traveler leaves the familiar hearth, he is intrigued and fascinated by the various cultures he encounters. As we go from one country to another, we are impressed by the differences in styles of dress, housing, food, the sound of languages and music, and the type of transportation and religious practices. In many countries we observe ways of life that are rooted in antiquity such as the rural areas of Egypt, for instance, where the peasant plows with water buffalo and a wooden plow. They may carry water from the well in earthen jars and in many ways life is not far removed from the time of the Pharaohs 5,000 years ago. Thus, travel is like a time machine. It helps us go back in time and examine how our ancestors responded to their environment. However, if we examine the interpersonal behavior of other cultures, we find it is very similar to our own. It is easy to allow the unfamiliar language and exotic customs to hide the fact that they are responding to life's problems with the same patterns of social response found in modern society.

In order to try to understand ourselves, let us take our time machine back millions of years. Examining the archeological and anthropological evidence in Africa suggests that our ancestors, called humanoids, probably split off from the other ape-like creatures about four million years ago and evolved along a separate line, as it were, up to our present form. The course followed by the great apes seems to have ended up in an evolutionary blind alley. In spite of this, startling discoveries at Stanford and at other primate centers recently have shown that a gorilla or a chimp, when trained to communicate by sign language, has many of the traits we long considered to be exclusively human.

The gorillas have learned to use vocabularies of 3 to 500 words. They can construct sentences, they are aware of past and future, they make value judgments, and they sometimes deliberately misbehave. Recently, a gorilla was found to have an IQ of 95. These similarities and behavioral characteristics that we share with the higher animals now seem to indicate that our emotions, our character traits, and our capacities are deeply rooted in our genetic material. In other words, we are pre-programmed.

Our environment, of course, alters the outcome, but only within the limits of our genetic capacities. Recent studies of primitive and modern people show that facial expressions and gestures related to the basic emotions are identical in almost every race. These gestures can also be recognized in the primates. Therefore, the inherited DNA and protein structure of our brain cells organize our ideas, emotions, and behaviors into predictable patterns.

We now know that in all creatures anxiety is generated when things don't conform to the familiar. How good we feel with people, places, and ideas that we understand. Familiar things generate security. Common emotional needs account for cultural similarities. These cultural practices eventually become dogma or laws, and variants from these laws in many cultures call for punishment. Punishment, then, satisfies a need in a group because it preserves the familiar, comfortable, tried and true ways. But within the security of these groups there is also a need for individuality or identity. This individuality is manifested to a greater degree in man than in more primitive creatures or even in the apes. This search for identity required a certain amount of tolerance from the group, and tolerance within a group was by necessity limited in primitive cultures. In early history, as well as in our living primitive cultures, the welfare of the group itself was always given priority, thus the logic of human sacrifice. This common practice was often designed to appease the gods so that the group might receive some special favor.

This brings us to the Greeks. The idea of tolerance of individuality really started with the Greeks. Pericles makes the statement that "organized society must protect freedom of behavior for its individual members." Fifty years later, Socrates, according to his student Plato, spent his life teaching tolerance and encouraging thought divergent from everyday doctrine. In his seventh epistle, he states, "All points of view have something to contribute to the understanding of the universe." Socrates, of course, drank hemlock as a reward for his promotion of individualism.

This brings me back to our recent trip to the Middle East. While in Athens, my Greek friend, Peter Bonoris, took Lera and me to the program entitled "Sounds and Lights." Many must have attended this. As we sat on a hill in the warm summer evening, we listened to the program describing the battles affecting the Athenians during the dominance of this unusual city. The lighting effect of the Acropolis and Parthenon was impressive. I couldn't help wonder, as I listened to the story of this fabled city, why their idealized democratic principles, now copied all over the Western world, have failed so badly in Greece. And why are these principles under such siege in many countries?

Later, while Lera and I were enjoying a meal at a typical Greek taverna with Peter and his wife, I put this question to our host. After a few minutes of thought, he said, "The idea is appealing, but it is a little impractical. Even though it was better suited to a small homogenous population (Athens had only 25,000 people in 600 B.C.), it was even then only applied selectively to the citizens. There are many slaves who were excluded from citizenship under Greek law."

We discussed the ways in which the Greek cult of the individual was adopted by Saul of Tarsus, the Assyrian Jew, and spread via the gospel of Christianity throughout the Western world. Although the Christian teachings emphasized our responsibility to our family and social group, as did the Greeks, the "rights" of the individual have taken more and more importance in recent times. These ideas have percolated up through our political and social systems and have recently become a major destructive force.

Democracy evolved philosophically in Greece in 600 G.C. and politically in the United States in 1776. Our Founding Fathers believed so strongly in the Judeo-Christian ethic of service to others and responsibility for the welfare of the group that they intuitively believed we would all conform to this idea because it was the natural order of things. But they also believed in the rights of the individual within these constraints. But with time, democracy has changed. Our children know democracy as a system that attempts to satisfy every want and every individual whim without regard for the welfare of the group. We don't even know who the group is, or if there is one. In Athens, the group constituted the citizens of their city. Today it might be no broader than the high school student body, the fans of the N.Y. Yankees, or the Black Eyed Peas.

At this time America has reached a pinnacle of achievement in many areas, but Peter, who had spent a year with us in the United States, wondered, and I agreed, if we have failed to demand a certain degree of responsibility as a price for our freedom. It appears that we have created a monstrous bureaucracy and transferred our individual responsibilities to this enormous uncontrollable octopus. In this way we seem to feel justified in abandoning our responsibilities to our friends and family, electing to act as dependent children seeking security in an all-powerful government. We are even willing to give up a good deal of our freedom in order to play a more passive role, and be somewhat removed from the consequences of our actions.

The proliferation of liability litigation, government subsidies, and abandonment of our concern for others, including our own families, is all a part of this trend. We might call our new system "democratic socialism with emphasis on instant gratification." Small wonder our children's perception of our social establishment is different than "us old folks," our Founding Fathers, or the Greeks.

When we consider these social trends and our new knowledge of anthropology, it becomes a little easier to understand the apparent deviant behavior of some of our adolescents. Studies of primitive cultures and habit patterns in animals tend to indicate that every son both loves and hates his father, that he has a biological need to go out and try his own wings, and often does this by gathering support from his peers. When this happens, the son is free to explore new cultures (the neighboring tribe or cult) and thus in primitive times crossbreeding was insured, which maintained the vitality of the race. These young Turks, however, turn out to be a threat to the father figure and to authority and thus often engender anger and fear in their elders. This behavior, dictated by our biology and the genetic basis for individualism, however, allows for the development of new concepts, and promotes the evolution of new cultures (environmentalism, anti-nuclearism, etc.). Some of the ideas are an improvement and some are not. We must all remember that none of these experiments in individualism can escape their source. They are circumscribed by the same drives, emotions, needs for approval, and limitations as are our older cultures. We should try to examine and understand these individualistic and nonconforming lifestyles in this light.

So, as we sat under the stars gazing at the Acropolis, the cradle of Western political and social ideology, I wondered if the United States was the culmination of this social experiment called democracy, which now may be in its downward trend, and if another ideology would appear and build a new culture or social order. With our present knowledge of physical laws, animal and human behavior, and scientific knowledge of biology, which provides a new understanding of history, we could be on the threshold of such a system.

We would hope this new system would not be based solely on hedonism or what seems desirable in a historical and popular sense, but would be based on a realistic understanding of our capacities and limitations to act so that our expectations will be in consort with our capabilities. The time is past when we can safely set up a dogmatic, rigid social system based on idealized beliefs of what we should be. We must again temper individualism with concern for our fellow man and our social groups, a trait that is part of our genetic makeup and the backbone of established religious and social systems for thousands of years. We must carefully weigh our new knowledge about man, his capacities, his limitations, and his social institutions and bite the bullet and face up to what we really are. After we have done this, and only then, a social order can be constructed from which to launch our next great leap forward, probably to achievements far beyond our present dreams.

CONFORMITY: THE SOCIETAL PRISON

There is a general belief that, although in the Dark Ages and before the behavior of humans was often irrational, being influenced by superstition and mythical beliefs, those days are in the past.

We, theoretically, have learned, as the years go by, that by logically analyzing facts, we can avoid many of the foolish beliefs of our forefathers and make rational decisions that are based on the discoveries of science and technology. We believe our present civilization is the most advanced in history. Those who have received advanced formal education are confident that the important decisions are the product of a logical analysis of the facts. Considering the enormous increase in information available, we should be able to make fewer mistakes and be able to work together to foster the common good.

About five or six thousand years ago our ancestors, many of whom were still hunter-gatherers, lived in small groups and discovered that working together was the most efficient way to survive and prosper. As these social groups enlarged, it became obvious that success required that they all conformed to similar rules and customs. It is likely that evolution favored those who conformed and that religions evolved to induce conformity. Although history concentrates on stories about nonconformists, the heroes, and unusual events, almost everyone learned that survival required conformity, even though the nonconformists were interesting, had ideas that favored progress, and, in many cases, were idolized but in some cases were demonized.

As we study ancient civilization while traveling around the globe, it is surprising how little has changed.

Those depicted in the Greek statues do not look too much different from people on the streets of Athens. When we visit China, the Chinese young people wear blue jeans, as do those in the United States and Germany. When we compare the stories of the Trojan wars, the logic for going to war is little different than our wars of today. The political systems people select, many of which have been demonstrated to be failures, have been selected repeatedly. Popular music is surprisingly similar in many cultures. Millions go to gambling casinos, even though they always lose money.

The examples I have listed are not stratified by education or income or country of origin or intelligence.

When I drive down the residential street where I live, the similarity of the houses and landscaping reinforces the need

Appendix and Essays

for conformity. When I discuss politics, it is remarkable how all academics are Democrats and Protestant religious groups are Republicans.

The downside of the urge to conform is that it seems as powerful today as it was 4,000 years ago, in spite of our progress in technology, education, and material prosperity.

Consider all of the religious wars, the millions of people who have been murdered because they failed to conform. Consider all of the progress that has been derailed because an idea was new.

In spite of all the scientific proof, less than half of Americans believe in evolution. Darwin postponed publication of his theory for over twenty years because it did not conform to the religious beliefs of the period. William Harvey, who proved blood circulated, also delayed publishing Du Motu Cordis for many years because it did not conform to the teachings of Galen that held sway for 500 years.

Today, in medicine, we are urged to *get with the guidelines* in patient management. Political plans to reform our healthcare will be based on requirements that we all conform to regulations decided by the government.

Humans have a powerful need to conform, to be alike, look alike, and do what others in their social group do. Many times this urge leads to destruction and human suffering. Is there a cure for this disease? It's been around for thousands of years. It seems incurable.

My parting comment: Blessed is he that is politically incorrect. Although he will have torrents of derision heaped on his head, his efforts will shed much light in dark corners. We need more nonconformists.

Some disturbing information about conformity should be mentioned.

It is obvious that those who commit crimes are nonconformists, are selfish, and socially looked down upon. Yet, their impact on society is miniscule compared to the death and destruction resulting from loyalty to a cause, a government, or a religion. The willingness to kill or die for a cause or a leader has been, throughout history, well documented by Stanley Milgram. An experiment done at Yale University a few years ago sheds some light on the subject.

Dr. Milgram was interested in understanding the limits of the average person's obedience to authority. It involved three people: the authority (a professor in a white coat), a learner or victim, and an experimental subject who was directed by the professor to punish the learner for his mistakes when giving the wrong reply to a question. The punishment for the wrong answers was electric shocks, gradually increased in voltage with each mistake. Although the meter registering the voltage was visible to everyone, only the volunteer (the teacher) did not know they were a fake. Each time the teacher (the experimental subject) was directed by the professor to increase the voltage, the student would cry out in pain, louder and with more anguish as the voltage was increased. Eventually, the voltage would be increased from 75 volts to 350 volts, resulting in louder screams. Although the teacher (the experimental subject) usually hesitated to increase the voltage, he was commanded to do so by the professor.

Although the "teachers" were volunteers, receiving a small stipend for their cooperation, as the student continued to give the wrong answer, they usually continued to increase the voltage, in spite of the screams of the learner.

It turns out that 60% of the subjects continued to obey the professor until the maximum 350 volts, in spite of the screams of the learner.

How is it that the professor continued to impose his authority on the "teacher"? The act of shocking the victim was not because the teacher was basically bad but because he had become integrated into a social structure he could not bring himself to abandon.

The experimental subjects did not receive pleasure from inflicting pain and most implored the professor to allow them to quit, but when denied this request, they continued to increase the strength of the shocks.

Thus, ordinary individuals, without any hostility, can be influenced to commit destructive acts when submitting to authority, even when it transcends their sense of morality.

Similar experiments in several centers have confirmed the results of the Yale group. Conformity with the group or with a perceived authority seems to be part of our nature. Thus, the explanation for many of our atrocities and for why we conform to societal standards and behavior is provided. This acceptance of authority may be the result of our long period of childhood dependency where we learn to conform to a parent's wishes who provide for our needs, for love and food during the formative years. Should we try to overcome this need or accept that its overall benefit is worth the cost?

Conclusions

The stories and ideas included in this little book should lead us to believe that ideas are not only interesting but suggest that we consider that they can change our culture, change our understanding, and help us adjust to the world and society. In the Middle Ages, there was a general belief that almost all significant ideas had come from the ancients. To be educated you had to have learned what Socrates, Galen, and other recognized sages had revealed. Although we have learned a lot from studying history, new ideas, as well as those in the past, are changing the way we live. I think this is happening more rapidly than at any time in history.

Our acceptance in the United States of new ideas was probably because we were a young society without an established history or dogma. This led to a new form of government, new attitudes about interpersonal relationships, and new ways of doing business. I believe new ideas were the reason a primitive society evolved to be the most successful, the most affluent, and the leader in science and technology in a little over 200 years.

We now know that combining information from many sources leads us to new ways of thinking. Can we convince our youth that appreciation of the ideas that came from the past, combined with the innovations of the present, will reveal a new reality? Possibly new concepts that will make life better for us all? Some people might consider these stories a form of philosophy. Maybe some of the ideas presented will be worth incorporating into the way you think and relate to events and to those who are important in your life.

Many people would rather not consider ideas that they disagree with. Richard Holmes, author of an interesting book *Age of Wonder*, said, "Scientific discoveries are as unexpected and interesting as poetry. The boundless prodigality of nature inspired scientists and poets with the same feelings of wonder." I feel the same way about ideas, which lead to discoveries in science, in society, in business, and in our understanding of each other.

Books

Listed are a few of my favorite books, the sources of some of my ideas:

1. *The Richness of Life.* Stephen Jay Gould. Norton & Company
2. *Eight Little Piggies.* Stephen Jay Gould. Norton & Company
3. *A World of Ideas.* Bill Moyers. Doubleday
4. *Facts and Ideas from Anywhere.* Futura Publishing
5. *Conscience.* Edward O. Wilson. Alfred Knoff
6. *The Science of Good and Evil.* Michael Shermer. Times Books
7. *Confucius: A Biography.* Jonathan Clements. Sutton Publishing Gloucester
8. *Physics of the Future.* Michio Kaku. Doubleday

9. *The Philosophical Breakfast Club.* Laura Snyder. Random House

10. *Where Good Ideas Come From.* Steven Johnson. Penguin Books

11. *American Prometheus.* Robert Oppenheimer. Kai Bird & M.J. Sherwin

12. *The Double Helix.* James Watson. Simon & Schuster

13. *The Spirit of Invention.* Smithsonian Books

14. *Adventures of Ideas.* Alfred Whitehead. Free Press

15. *The Language of Life.* Francis Collins. Harper-Collins

16. *Lateral Thinking.* Edward de Bono. Harper

17. *The Innovators DNA.* J. Dyer, H. Gregerson, C. Christensen. Harvard Business Review

18. *The Great Experiment.* Strobe Talbott. Simon & Schuster

19. *The Death of Common Sense.* Philip K. Howard. Random House

20. *The Microtheory of Innovative Entrepreneurship.* William Baumol. Princeton University Press

21. *Mendel in 90 Minutes.* John and Mary Gribbin. Constable & Co.

22. *The Morality of Capitalism.* Tom Palmer, Jameson Books

23. *What's Wrong With Benevolence.* David Stove, Encounter Books

Appendix and Essays

24. *Good and Evil.* Michael Shermer, Times Books
25. *Decoding the Language of God.* George Cunningham, Prometheus Books
26. *Three Seductive Ideas.* Jerome Kagan, Harvard University Press
27. *The Great Thoughts.* George Seldes, Ballantine Books
28. *Rock the Casbah.* Robin Wright
29. *Janus: A Summing Up.* Arthur Koestler

Acknowledgments

This book was suggested by my lovely daughter, Cheryl Warren, and typed by my long-term friend and secretary, Carole Sweet. Donna Reckseen helped with editing, and Michael Levin provided welcomed advice.

www.myrvinellestad.com

www.ingramcontent.com/pod-product-compliance
Lightning Source LLC
Chambersburg PA
CBHW061658040426
42446CB00010B/1796